DON'T SETTLE FOR A LESSER LIFE IN YOUR LATER YEARS

JOHN WINDSOR

CONTENTS

Appendix

To my amazing clients, who continue to inspire me.

And to Katrin, Bryan, and Dan,
who make life worth living.

Introduction

For such a provocative title, this book had an innocent birth. A new client came to see me for coaching on what to do when she ended her 30-year career. Only she didn't want to retire, not in the traditional sense. She was a top executive at a prominent company and she loved the challenge of work. In her early 60s, she still competed in marathons and traveled extensively. She was bursting with life — until she said the word "retire," and then it was like watching a balloon deflate.

I said to her, "This word is creating problems. We need to say 'fuck retirement' and find a new way to think about what's ahead of you." We decided to call this Version 2 of her life. That changed her attitude immediately. It also created the spark for this book.

The *F*ck Retirement* mindset does not require you to keep working until your final days. Some people will want to, or need to, but that's not what this book proposes. It's about making the most of your life at any age, in whatever way you design it, and with the greatest longevity you can achieve.

So whether you said "Hell, Yes" when you read the title or "Hell, No," this book is for you. Whether you want to create the next big chapter in your life or you want a permanent vacation — or you don't know what the hell you want — this book is for you.

If you're in the "Hell, Yes" camp, this book will help you figure out a new direction, something that can inspire and sustain you for years. You'll develop a plan for reinventing your life and put it into action, and you'll learn how to deal with the various challenges that are likely to arise. And, because you can't avoid dealing with ageism and old thinking patterns that could hold you back, you'll get a mental reset on what retirement and aging are really about, and how best to optimize your life.

If you're in the "Hell, No" camp, life does not become perfect and worry-free when you retire. You may experience physical and mental declines, you'll have to deal with ageism, and you'll battle limiting beliefs that you've carried since childhood. The choices you make now can either increase your longevity or destroy it. This book will show you the right path to a longer, healthier life, whether you want to reinvent yourself or not.

If you're somewhere between "Hell, Yes" and "Hell, No" — like if retirement seems a long way off — do not put this book down. Most of us have been programmed since we were toddlers to believe that older people are dull, drab, frail, and sad. Those images are changing, but that doesn't help anyone who grew up in the 1980s or earlier. So learning to pay attention now to your language and changing your mindset about what's to come in your later years will put you on a better track to having a long, happy, healthy, and even badass time through the rest of your life.

And if you're confused about what retirement really means to you, welcome aboard. You'll find no better resource for figuring out this puzzle, both the "retirement" part and how to live a full, dynamic life to the end of your days.

This book has two parts: *Rethinking Retirement & Aging* and *Reinventing Yourself.* The first part exposes misconceptions about retirement and aging, and the insidious ways ageism creeps in. It shines a light on what retirement really is, how our beliefs about retirement and aging have been shaped, and how you can optimize your life to make the most of every day. Included in this section are chapters on *"Oh, Shit!" Moments in Aging* and *How to Be a Badass in Your 80s & 90s.* If you only read that far, and you do the exercises, you'll get life-changing value out of this book.

In *Reinventing Yourself,* the book takes you further, through the five phases of change required to transform your life. You'll establish the baseline of where you are now, do brainstorming exercises that move you way beyond what you might have imagined for yourself, create the steps to launch your new chapter, and learn how to deal with all the forces trying to sink your efforts.

My intention with this book is to help you change your life, in ways small and large. It isn't just a review of what's happening in the world of retirement and aging, it's a let's-get-shit-done-so-your-life-is-better-than-ever-(at-any-age) program. So along with the anti-ageist rallying, this gives you a step-by-step workbook to guide your path to real, sustainable change. Throughout the book you'll find questions designed to get you to think deeply about your life, along with space in which to write your answers. *Don't skip over them!* If you're serious about change, you have to do the work. There's no magic dust I can shoot out of these pages to eliminate the effort.

If you have any thoughts about being too old to do this work, push those aside right now. You are not too old — you are never too old — unless you choose to believe that you are. You'll meet lots of people in this book who will prove that to you. And while ageism and the ravages of time might seem like formidable foes, there are always alternatives to be explored. Consider this example:

One of my clients is a chaired professor and prominent scientist. After more than 30 years in academia, he knows there will be an end to what he's been doing; if nothing else, the process of winning grants is getting harder and administrative demands have become a burden. But he still *loves* doing science! There's no way he wants to stop, and there's no reason he should have to, since he keeps getting smarter and more creative with each year. He lights up when he talks about his work. So his goal is to find a new direction that allows him to stay lit up — to be challenged, pushed, stymied, inspired, involved, and to continue to make a significant contribution to science and to the world.

If you want to stay lit up, if you want to live life on *your* terms, if you want to feel *involved* to the end of your days, this book is for you.

Even if your knees creak, you take a bunch of pills, and you've got lines and lumpiness everywhere, it's not evidence that you're past your prime. Your brain may process some things differently, but it has also gained superpowers that younger brains have yet to attain. Most of all, your spirit still holds the spark of joy and life that make living so vital, and that is *ageless*. Even if you feel like your spirit has been beaten down — IT'S STILL THERE.

Let's go find it and keep that fire inside you burning.

Rethinking Retirement & Aging

Your 40s are good.
Your 50s are great.
Your 60s are fab.
And 70 is fucking awesome!

· Dame Helen Mirren ·
(still working)

Attitudes About Retirement

"Just hand me the rope!"

I did not expect that reaction the first time I asked someone what the word "Retirement" meant to him. My friend Paul barked it out. "Just hand me the rope!" he said, and then pretended to hang himself. Yikes!

I eventually talked to hundreds of people about their attitudes regarding retirement and reinvention; that's what this chapter explores. But it's not just a casual stroll through people's opinions. There are lessons to be learned from current attitudes and approaches.

While I met more people like Paul, there were also many who were giddy at the prospect of being freed from work life as they'd known it. Rachel shared her dream of lounging around in oversized silk pajamas, sipping coffee and wondering about the day — *Read a book? Go to a flea market?* — sharing cocktails with friends, flying around the country, and getting in touch with her spiritual side. She hasn't retired yet, but she knows what she wants when the time comes. If we ran a poll, we'd likely get millions of people longing for something similar.

Or Beth, who taught school for over 30 years and is now blissfully happy to wake up in the morning and have no idea what she's going to do that day. She's only a couple years into retirement, so it remains to be seen if she's still as blissful in ten years. Maybe she will be, or maybe she'll get restless and find something to jump into with a timeline longer than a few days. For the moment, though, she's happy, happy, happy.

And there are some for whom retirement is their deliverance from a lifetime of drudgery in a job that paid their bills but gave them nothing else. As Dave said, "Whatever retirement is like, it will be an improvement on my life right now." A lot of people with this mindset are content just living for today.

Others, however, don't have the luxury of retiring. We'll talk about this more in a little bit.

Then there are those who seem to be speeding up, rather than slowing down. They feel like time is a diminishing resource and there's still so much to do. That brings a sharp focus and a sense of purpose to their days.

One of my uncles is a good example. As my cousin wrote, his dad became busier than ever after he retired — joined the local economic town council, became active in the management of their yacht club, managed the finances of the neighborhood association, was an active sailor who set racing markers and ran the crash boat — the list goes on and on. At 87, my uncle has eased up a little, but he's still extremely active. My cousin finished with this reflection on his dad: "I guess you could say he started living his life."

And some people are still having so much fun at their careers that they have no desire to stop working and aren't being forced out. John Goodenough is still working as a mechanical engineering professor at the University of Texas at Austin. In 2019, he shared the Nobel Prize for Chemistry for helping develop the lithium-ion battery. Aged 97 at the time, he became the oldest person to be awarded a Nobel Prize, *and he's still doing research!* What a beacon of potential is he.

In between the archetypes — Hate Retirement, Love Retirement, and What's Retirement? — are lots of flavors of "Yes, I want this (but)" and "No, I reject that (but)."

Yes, I want a break from what I've been doing. Yes, I want to be free from the drudgery I've lived through. Yes, I want to live life on my terms, and if I want to lounge all day, yay for me! Yes, I want to travel and paint and see friends and play golf and learn to play the tuba and (on and on and on), *BUT I also want to do something meaningful.*

Or . . .

No, I don't want to take a back seat. No, I don't want to buy into the idea that I'm old or less-than in any way. No, I'm not suddenly addled-brained or incompetent. No, I'm not through building incredible things and trying to shake up the world, BUT I also want to lounge around when I want.

My wife provides a perfect example.

She said to me, "It's pretty strange that my husband is writing a book called *F*ck Retirement* and, with all I've got going on, retirement sounds really appealing."

I would bet money, however, that when that day arrives she won't know what to do with herself. We had a test-run 20 years ago and she failed miserably at it.

Until our sons left for college, we always had one of us at home, taking care of them but also doing business work of some type; the first stay-at-home parent was me. While watching the boys, I was also writing novels. After a few years, my wife decided she'd had enough of the corporate life and announced that it was time to switch roles; she wanted more time with the kids and more time for herself.

I was able to convert a consulting gig into a full-time position, so on the appointed day, I drove off to start my new job. And my wife suddenly had the freedom she'd so deeply desired.

After I left, she got the boys off to preschool and then had the day to herself. She could now do anything she wanted. Or she could do nothing at all. She could drive to the beach, have coffee with friends, spend all day in the bookstore, or just lie in the middle of the living room for hours and watch patterns of light shift across the walls.

How long did her new life of leisure last?

Two hours.

Then she plunged into developing new business ideas, making lists of people she should talk to, and even designing a logo for the new company she was going to launch.

Some people can't slow down, even when given the opportunity. My wife and I are both afflicted with that, actually.

The Italians have a concept called "far niente," which means to do nothing. It's the standard approach for many people's beach vacations — just sand, sea, lounge chair, and fruity drinks for hours.

We'd never been successful at that, but on a trip to Sicily years ago, we decided that *this time* we were going to JUST.CHILL.OUT. The first morning, we went to the beach, got our sons situated in the sea, and laid back in our assigned beach chairs to begin far nient-ing.

It lasted 20 minutes. Then we both popped out of our chairs and said, "Let's *do* something!"

I haven't seen scientific studies on this, but there's a good chance that how you approach your vacations is how you're likely to approach your later years. Are you looking for a leaf-peeping life or soul-stirring exploits? Do you envision mulled wine on slow boat rides or a tequila-infused romp through new lands and challenging adventures?

It's okay to want both, of course. But my guess is that people tend to lean one way or the other when it comes to major life transitions, either easing into them or plunging headlong into the void.

So what really speaks to you? An easy, passive life where you reap the fruits of your labors and are happy to let others do the heavy lifting? Or an active, What-new-thing-can-I-do-next kind of existence? Are you more interested in Comfortable and Familiar, or Uncertain and Surprising?

It's important to consider this now, because if you want a leaf-peeping life, you might not be inclined to do the deep work that reinvention requires. And that's cool. Just finish this first section and then hang onto the book in case you get restless later.

To take this Passive v. Active distinction further, let's look at what science tells us about what makes people happy. In his landmark book, *Flow: The Psychology of Optimal Experience,* Mihaly Csikszentmihalyi found that the best moments in our lives are not the passive, receptive, relaxing times. "The best moments," he wrote, "usually occur when a person's body or mind is stretched to its limits in a voluntary effort to accomplish something difficult or worthwhile."

He doesn't say that we're *not* happy when we're passive, receptive, and relaxed — but we're happiest when we're engaged in something that challenges us, where we're called upon to grow, and perhaps to add meaning to the world.

The one consistent theme among those I asked about retirement was "Possibilities." Possibilities to do new things, to explore new lands, to channel their energies in different ways, and so on. It should be noted that the people who talked the most about possibilities tended to be in the ranks of the not-yet-retired or the newly-retired — people who were eager for the change or just getting started in their new direction.

James is a great example of this. After 25 years in major roles with a big consumer product goods company, he retired — at age 48 — to begin a new career as an executive coach. He happily wears the mantle of "retired," but he hasn't stopped working. He's just doing something different now that really inspires him, and he's able to set his schedule to be as full or as light as he likes. And while he relishes having more free time in his day, he's also developing some really interesting projects that give him the chance to have an impact on the world in very different ways than when he was traveling the globe marketing soft drinks.

Would you call that "retired?" If not, what would you call it?

James's experience is important for a couple reasons — timing and control.

Timing speaks to *when* you make a big change in your life. Are you ready for it or has change been thrust upon you? When you can choose the date, the transition is easier to manage. It might even be fun and something to look forward to. At the very least, it can help you better organize your life.

One of my clients was really struggling with his situation at work. He'd been with the same company for 30 years and knew he could stay on indefinitely if he felt like it. But he wanted to leave at some point, and on his own terms. The problem was deciding when. The projects he led had multi-year arcs, so he couldn't just walk out tomorrow, and he still enjoyed many aspects of his work. His uncertainty about when to leave was causing a lot of stress.

I challenged him to set a date for leaving his company, and gave him three days to decide. Once he made his choice, he felt like a major burden had been lifted. It made it easier for him to be all-in with his current projects, while also beginning to plan his next phase. Clarity is a wonderful thing.

Implicit in setting a date is having control of your transition. Being able to decide when, where, and how you'll finish your current job lessens the feelings of fear, uncertainty, and doubt about what you're facing. It leaves you hopeful about your future and more ready to tackle what's coming.

But sometimes outside factors rob you of control or force decisions on you. The pandemic has been a major influence here. Businesses closed, workers were furloughed or laid off, and most of us had to figure out how to work from home without losing our minds. As we've come out of the pandemic, a large percentage of people are not returning to business as it used to be.

This has prompted some people to take an early retirement, having put away enough money to support themselves. Either they don't want to return to the work environment they used to know or, because of the pandemic, they have a new perspective on what really matters to them. While they are leaving with a new sense of freedom, they are likely to hit a dip in a year or two, if they haven't already figured out what the next chapter of their life will be.

Those I-might-as-well-retire folks are dwarfed by the legions of people who were battered during the pandemic. Whether it's because of a loss of their job, few prospects for new employment, reduced unemployment support, ongoing health issues, or huge medical bills, many had to dip into their savings or their retirement funds just to survive. The lack of control for this group is particularly harsh, and no amount of cheerleading or feel-good messages is likely to help.

The situation is exacerbated when the stench of ageism is present. Trying to get a new job when you've been in the workforce for 20 or 30 years was difficult *before* the pandemic and it's only worse now. I'll have more on this in a moment.

Another prominent theme was around Purpose, about having a reason why you do (or will do) the things you do; many people described this as having a reason to get out of bed in the morning. Few people I talked to had grand plans for changing the world, but many of them talked about making a contribution of time, energy, and expertise to special groups or communities. They saw retirement as a time to give back or to get involved in passion projects that their prior schedule couldn't allow. As with my uncle, this work might follow many paths.

A common answer about purpose came in supporting one's family, especially in caring for grandchildren. I haven't graduated to Grandpa status, but I get the attraction, having spent time with a niece's babies. And this kind of engagement is a powerful bonding experience for everyone — grandparents, their children, and their grandchildren. I'm 100% in on this as a way to find purpose in your life.

But is it enough? If you're living mostly for your kids or grandkids, and otherwise whiling away the hours — a book club here, a fishing trip there, dinners with friends, Netflix or SportsCenter running constantly on the TV — you may be missing out on sharing all the other gifts you have to give to the world, whether that world has a radius of five miles or five thousand miles.

Your health and longevity may be at risk, too, if there's not something to which you're dedicating your energies. Psychology professor Eric Kim found that having a higher sense of purpose is correlated with a reduced risk of disability, stroke, heart disease, and sleep issues. And gerontologist Ross Andel suggests we may be at risk of cognitive decline if we don't have the kind of mental activity we had when we were working.

The last thing of note from all my conversations about retirement concerns language: how people talk about this time in their life. For all the euphemisms I've heard and read about aging and reinvention — Your Third Act, Rewired, Encore careers, and more — the people I talked to almost universally called it "retirement." That's still a loaded word to many of us, though it's infinitely better than "Seniors" or "the Elderly."

Among the most prominent writers on retirement and reinvention, there is not a common agreement on language. Each author seems to have her or his own spin for this time of life. And some of them are in disagreement about it. Chip Conley in *Wisdom@Work* talks about becoming a "Modern Elder," conferring wisdom on those who've lived a lot, seen a lot, experienced a lot. Ashton Applewhite in *This Chair Rocks: A Manifesto Against Aging*, however, prefers "Olders" or "Old

Person in Training" to "Elders," since she objects to people deserving respect purely because of their age.

The big lesson here is about labels. We are hardwired to label things, including ourselves, and we're often quick to accept the labels that other people put on us. Labels help us categorize and simplify the world around us.

Labels aren't necessarily bad, unless you limit yourself based on the meanings you've attached to these labels. And limiting yourself in any part of your life *is* bad, because it robs you of the richness and possibilities that could make your life and the lives of the people you touch even better.

That said, some labels can be fun. One I'm adopting is *The Howard Beale of Aging*, after the character from the movie *Network*, who famously shouted, "I'm as mad as hell and I'm not going to take it anymore!" It may be a little obscure, but it gives me license to show up in powerful ways, and that's when labels *can* be helpful — when we choose how to think about ourselves and how to be in this world.

The superpower is to not dwell on labels at all. With respect to Ashton Applewhite, Chip Conley, and everyone else who has written about aging, what if we talk instead about *Being* — not being older or wiser, just being. After all, in the arc of your life, you accumulate day after day and experience after experience. There's not a magic (or evil) moment when a switch is flipped and you're suddenly older or wiser; you're just *You* on the next day.

If you really need a way to talk about this time in your life or in others' lives, how about your "second half" or your "third act?" That respects the dimension of time, which is the only true distinction among the ages, and reduces the likelihood of slapping a label on someone or on this rich new time of possibilities. (There's more in the next two chapters about the words we use and their impact.)

What If You Can't Retire?

If you don't feel free to pursue a different life, the last thing you need is for me to bounce around chanting, "You've GOT this! You can do it! You can beat <whatever is holding you back>!" What you probably need — other than a new job, a wonder drug, relief care, or maybe winning the lottery — is someone who will listen, who will hear you without judgment, and not try to fix you or bury you in wise sayings.

It's a little hard for me to do via a book, but I see you. I know you're angry or dejected or otherwise suffering. I don't have simple answers or "The 10 Guaranteed Steps to Getting Out of Your Rut!" This book is no shiny object that will magically change your life.

You *can* change your life, but the magic comes from you, not me or anyone else.

The question now is how you feel about your situation, and how you'd *like to feel* about it. Whether you continue to work because you don't have enough money saved, you need the benefits your employer provides, your funds have been obliterated by pandemic-related issues, or you're paying off debts, you can still choose how you want to feel. You can choose the stories you tell yourself.

It may be hard to imagine this when it seems like you are trapped, but you *can* take control of your thoughts. I'm not suggesting you should suddenly be ecstatic about having to work or being overloaded with debt, but choosing to be something other than miserable is a great first step.

This book has ideas that can help you shift your perspective, but it doesn't have answers — *you* have the answers. The problem is that the answers, ideas, and changes in outlook that will help you are hidden under years or even a lifetime of harsh messages, tough experiences, negative programming, and more.

I don't mention this to make you wrong. You will not hear me say, "Snap out of it" or "What do you have to complain about?" Judgments are the last thing you need.

But there is always some room for shifting your situation, even in bleak moments. That shift may not come gift-wrapped with a mansion on the hill, but if you're open to having a life other than what you feel stuck in right now, there *is* some kind of way.

How do you make that shift? That's what this book is about. What would that shift look like? You'll find out, and probably be surprised, by doing the work set out in these pages.

Will this book solve your money woes? No, only you can do that. *You* have to do the work. *You* have to take a hard look at your situation and maybe make some difficult choices. *You* have to get uncomfortable — in ways you've perhaps avoided in the past.

This is my cue to share a story. Early in my coaching career, I had a client who wanted to make a change in his life. He had done some significant and successful things in his career, but he felt trapped where he was. Complicating his situation was that he had just turned 61 and had grave doubts about his ability to find a compelling new job in this age of ageism. He was tied in knots and didn't see any way clear.

As we worked together, we tapped into what really drove him, what unique gifts he had to offer the world, and to the spark of life that had once been so present and powerful, but had become buried under years of responsibility, expectations, and the limiting stories he had been telling himself.

There was also a shadow element lurking below the surface, something not seen or specific, that would sometimes rise up out of his gut and lead him to say "I'm not comfortable with that."

This didn't happen every session, but ultimately this feeling of being uncomfortable was a significant block for him. It kept him from making breakthroughs that could transform his life.

That realization was so clear, at least to me. If he stepped into his discomfort, he was going to find ways past it and have a freer life. He was going to be able to look at his situation with fresh eyes and become more intentional about his choices.

Where I failed him was in not being direct about this. I should have invited him *into* the discomfort to see what it could reveal, rather than letting him shut it all down with a terse "I'm not comfortable with that." This was early in my career and I hadn't had a lot of experience yet with clients confronting such significant blocks. So I shied away from inviting him into the uneasiness zone and eventually the coaching relationship ended with him still buffering against discomfort.

That was then, this is now.

If you want to change your situation, there is no painless way to do it; you would have done it already if there was. You have to examine your circumstances and then do something about them, as challenging as that may be, and not merely hope that change is gifted to you in a thunderbolt of good fortune. If you've worked on turning things around in the past but didn't see success, it's time to do this again.

You have to put aside any thoughts of being a victim, whether a victim of circumstance, bad decisions, or another's actions or words. I realize things may be bad for some people reading this, but rolling up in a ball of victimhood doesn't help. It just makes your world smaller and more painful.

I'm not suggesting you should adopt a power pose, throw your head back, and sing "The sun will come out ... tomorrow!" at the top of your lungs.

Just don't give up your ability to choose, even if the choices seem limited. Start small, make one little shift — and then another, and another, until you begin to see daylight. Maybe that means you start a side business, or join a spiritual or community circle, or create an advocacy group to help people like you who feel trapped. Anything that shifts you out of feeling stuck or beaten down is a positive step.

And if your path in your later years doesn't include months-long beach vacations or river cruises, so what? You're not a failure at life if you don't have an old-school retirement. A lot of us don't want that anyway. In a study by AgeWave/Edward Jones, only 22% of the retirees they surveyed saw retirement as a time for rest and relaxation; over half saw it as a new chapter in life. You don't need to retire to create something new for yourself.

If you need an example of persevering under horrible, life-and-death circumstances, check out Viktor Frankl's epic book, *Man's Search for Meaning*. In it, he describes his experiences in Nazi death camps during World War II. He and others survived wretched conditions and daily threats of death by reminding themselves of what they had to live for and why their lives had meaning.

While you're busy not-giving-up, be patient with yourself and the process. We're talking about a big change, and that takes time. As well, be kind to yourself. These are not the moments to beat yourself up or otherwise judge yourself. Exercise some self-compassion, in whatever way feels best. A long walk in nature? Meditation? A hard run on the trails? Whatever it is that gets you back to your center, use it.

What If You're Content Already?

So you've got Retirement nailed? Yay you! Just because I've written a book called *F*ck Retirement* doesn't mean I'm against traditional plans for retirement. My greatest hope is for everyone to live as fully as possible, no matter what shape that takes. It is not my intention to tell you you're wrong or missing something if you want a typical, never-work-again retirement, or that I have the real answers and you're a brainwashed dodo if you don't blow everything up. If you're happy with your life and retirement, I really am glad for you. Just keep it going. Don't shift anything if you're not feeling called to — and if you're not feeling called to change, you won't get into the depths this books asks of you.

But pay attention every now and then, not to what you're doing, but to how you're feeling. Is your life a 10? Maybe a 7 with occasional bursts to 10 and to 3? Or maybe you're at a 5, but you can't change your circumstances so it's best just to be happy with what you've got?

I've asked a lot of people who are already retired how they're feeling. The answers range from "I'm bored" to "I'm doing GREAT!" Generally, people say they're happy to be retired, as though it's all good, everything is settled, nothing-to-see-here-folks.

That's true for some people and not true for others, even if they profess to "having it made." Consider the story of a man profiled in a piece in the New York Times.

In an article titled *Taking Ayahuasca When You're A Senior Citizen*, Casey Schwartz explored the experiences of older people taking this psychedelic potion as a means to unlock things from their past and in their mind that, despite all their accomplishments in life, had left them unsatisfied.

Schwartz began the piece describing George Sarlo, a prominent venture capitalist in San Francisco. At 74, Sarlo had a beautiful home with incredible views of the Golden Gate Bridge and likely everything he needed for a comfortable life. Yet he was so unsettled by things from his youth that he went to a small Mexican village to seek the help of a shaman in unlocking his past.

Taking ayahuasca is said to be violently uncomfortable, and Sarlo needed two rounds to find the answers he sought, but for him it was worth it. He left the jungle with a new understanding of his past and a greater sense of peace that all his money and success had not been able to provide him. The article went on to cover many other stories and insights from health professionals; it's a fascinating read.

The point of this thread is not to say "Try ayahuasca!" nor to insinuate that things are not rosy in your life. Instead, it's to remind you to pay attention to how you're feeling, like a check-up for your soul. And if you sense anything other than rainbows and unicorns inside, give yourself permission to explore that and permission to change things if you find you're not satisfied.

You only get one life. Live it as fully as you can.

Below is the first of many exercises in this book. Please take the time to do them. Your greatest discoveries will come in the work you do on these prompts.

What are your biggest takeaways from this chapter?

What Is Retirement Anyway?

What's in a name? That which we call a rose
by any other name would smell as sweet.
· William Shakespeare ·

Though we've seen widely varying attitudes, from "I can't wait for retirement" to "I never want to retire," there seems to be agreement about the basic idea of what retirement is: a time, later in your life, when you are no longer working full-time in some kind of job. From that foundation, people paint their own picture of what retirement, in its full measure, means to them.

It's funny, though, that something regarded as a life phase, like adolescence and middle age (since "retirement" and "old age" cover roughly the same time), is a relatively recent idea, going back 150 years in its earliest forms. And the really juicy parts are even younger than that.

To help you better understand what retirement is and how best to navigate it, this chapter covers:

- A brief history of retirement
- Statistics about retirement
- Retirement issues in other countries
- A review of the language we use
- The stages of retirement

History

In 1871, German Chancellor Otto von Bismarck, through subtle diplomacy and sheer force of will, led the reunification of Germany, in what eventually became known as the Second Reich. Ten years later, however, the rise of the socialist movement had him worried. To protect his position, and to ward off calls for more radical socialist agendas, he preempted the Marxists with a social welfare program of his own.

His plan was to give a pension to any nonworking German over the age of 70. This had never been done before outside of the military, where payments to those who had served or compensation for families who had lost someone in battle dates back to Roman times. Pensions for the general population were a new thing.

It was rather brilliant from a policy perspective, since the average life expectancy of Germans at the time was 42. Bismarck could look like a man of the people by offering them monetary support, but the government would not have to pay out vast sums since few people reached the required age to start collecting.

It took German politicians eight years to finally enact this, but in 1889, "Retirement" was effectively born. They didn't use that word, and there's no record of when the word gained traction, but the first national program was in place. Over the course of the next 26 years, the German parliament reduced the starting age from 70 to 65.

Here in America, we also ended up at 65 for the age at which "old age" payments would start. When the Social Security program was being set up, it was initially pegged to begin at age 60. Since the average life expectancy at the time was 58 for men and 62 for women, that was more reasonable than Bismarck's scheme. But economic considerations led the framers of Social Security to set the starting age at 65. This was in line with most of the private and state-run programs that were popping up, and thus age 65 became the expected date at which retirement — and with it "old age" — should start.

None of these programs were created just to say, "We love you, older people! Thanks for all your hard work." Economics were at play.

The intention was to get older people out of the workforce so that younger people, at lower salary levels, could replace them.

There was also a common presumption that, once you reached a certain age — which typically was 60 — you no longer had the energy or brain capacity to be as productive or effective as you were when you were younger. Renowned physician William Osler, in 1905, declared that after age 60, the average worker was useless and should be put out to pasture.

When a lot of these programs were launched, however, the common reaction from those affected was not jubilation at being freed from a lifetime of work, but rather resistance. Older people weren't necessarily ready to stop working and resented being forced to.

The thing about all these programs, regardless of their initial intent, is that people *did* get something just for being older. And this created an entitlement mentality that persists today, the idea that we should get to retire, usually by age 65, and ideally with all our financial requirements taken care of.

> **Takeaway #1:** 65 years old is completely arbitrary as the age at which such a major life transition should happen. It could've been set at 74 or 63 or some other random number. So the age at which you plan your transition should be based on how you feel, how engaged you are with the work you're doing, and how inspired you may be about what's coming next in your life. (And how much money you've put away, if you intend to stop working for the rest of your days.)

Pensions aren't the only story here, however. There is an image of what retirement could be like that many of us grew up with, complete with sunny skies, beautiful surroundings, and a beaming white-haired couple radiating freedom and fun. Would it surprise you to know this is a manufactured ideal? Yep. The carefree lifestyle that seems synonymous with retirement is a concept that's only 60 years old. And it was born in a dusty cotton field 45 minutes outside of Phoenix, Arizona.

Del Webb was a real estate developer in the middle part of the 20th century, known initially for the government construction projects he led, including a Japanese-American internment camp in Arizona. He also built the Flamingo Hotel in Las Vegas for mobster Bugsy Siegel. This all made him rich enough to become a co-owner of the New York Yankees baseball club.

But in the late 1950s, he was looking for something bigger to do, something he could really put his stamp on. When he turned his gaze to the growing numbers of people retiring and moving to warmer climates, he got inspired.

In those days, the image of people aged 60 and older was one of decay, decline, and irrelevancy. Even Eleanor Roosevelt, who usually had smart things to say, suggested that older people are happy spending their days in their rocking chairs.

Del Webb, however, saw something different. He saw people who weren't ready to be hidden away, and who had money to spend. He also saw few enticing housing options for this group.

So he and his team dreamed up the first purpose-built, active-retirement community, complete with a shopping center, golf course, and recreation center for the 55+ crowd. He acquired land northwest of Phoenix and started construction. As they built five model homes and the rest of the infrastructure, his marketing and sales teams began to promote this new community.

Their promotional efforts were incredibly clever. This was the group that coined the phrase "Your Golden Years" to describe one's later life. And rather than just slap a title on the new community they were building, they ran a nationwide contest to pick a name. The winner: Sun City.

Sun City was unveiled on January 1, 1960. During the three-day opening weekend, more than 100,000 people visited the development, ten times more than what Del Webb and company expected. Nearly 300 homes were sold just that weekend, and Sun City and the revolution it started were so successful that Del Webb was selected as Time Magazine's Man of the Year in 1962.

The race was on to make retirement attractive, and "active lifestyle" retirement communities popped up all across the United States. As well, marketers for a dizzying array of products pumped out breathless copy and dazzling images of a perfect retirement.

Takeaway #2: The ideal of what retirement should be was dreamed up by marketers 60 years ago to sell houses. You do not have to buy into their pitch, no matter how many others hold onto those views. Write your own story of what your retirement can and should be.

Statistics

So is this idealized, Golden Years portrait of retirement as prevalent as it is prominent? Let's take a look.

- A 2020 study by AgeWave/Edward Jones found that only 22% of respondents considered retirement as "a time for rest and relaxation." More than half considered it "a new chapter in life." 15% considered it "a continuation of what life was," and 8% felt it was "the beginning of the end."

- A 2010 study on psychological research on retirement found that 75% of workers aged 50 and older expect to have a paid job during retirement.

- From a 2013 Bank of America Merrill Lynch/AgeWave study, when asked what the #1 key to happiness was, 81% said "Good Health," 58% said, "Financial Freedom," 36% said, "Family and Friends," and 20% said, "Purpose." (These numbers don't add up, but they're interesting insights nonetheless.)

- From that same study, when pre-retirees were asked about their biggest, expected loss in retirement, the #1 answer, at 38%, was "Reliable income." In a distant 2nd place, at 17%, was "Social connections." But when the same question was asked of people who had already retired, the #1 answer, at 34%, was "Social connections." In 2nd place was "Reliable income," which had dropped to 29%. And "Mental stimulation" rose from 12% for the pre-retirees to 19% for the retiree group.

▪ There's a trove of insights in a 2009 survey by Pew Research Center, entitled "Growing Old in America: Expectations v. Reality." They examined the responses of two cohorts: people aged 18-64 (55% of the total respondents) and people 65+ (45%). This gave them the chance to compare the younger group's expectations about life with the older group's actual experiences.

When it came to activities in retirement years, expectations did not match reality. Regarding having "More time with family," 86% of the younger cohort expected this, but only 70% of the older group agreed. For "Volunteer work," 80% was the expectation, but only 52% actually agreed. For "More travel," 77% of the younger group expected that; only 52% found that to be true.

▪ According to a 2013 study by the Institute of Economic Affairs, 40% of first-year retirees suffer from depression. In the 2nd year, that number rises to 50%. Psychologist say that it takes three years for the average retiree to figure out who they are outside the mainstream work world.

▪ There is not one definitive number for how many hours of TV a week is watched by the average American retiree. The results I've found range from 28 hours (four hours a day) to a whopping 48 hours of TV per week (nearly seven hours a day). And the total time in front of a screen has definitely increased as more and more older people use computers, smart phones and tablets to access social media, games, and internet applications.

The most important statistic I found in this regard is **five years**, as in "watching TV or videos for an average of six hours a day could shorten a viewer's life expectancy by five years," according to an Australian study. It's not so much the viewing that's the problem, but the sedentary lifestyle that accompanies it, which can lead to heart disease, diabetes, and obesity.

Takeaway #3: The image of a sunny retirement, as painted by marketers, misses the realities that most people experience. Sure, there may be times when you can just kick back, have a good time, and all your needs are met, but that's rarely a persistent state that spans 30 years or more. Sometimes it's hard. Sometimes it's messy. And uncertainties abound. So erase any expectations of what retirement *should* be and chart your own course.

Global Perspectives

According to a 2019 United Nations report on World Population Ageing [sic], "Population ageing is a human success story, a reason to celebrate the triumph of public health, medical advancements, and economic and social development over diseases, injuries, and early death that have limited human life spans throughout history."

Yay, us!

But few countries are cheering. Some are optimistic about it — in places where the proportion of older people is not growing as fast as the overall population, which includes the United States. In these countries, a younger labor force makes it possible to capitalize on development opportunities.

In many regions, however, particularly Europe and Southeast Asia, the proportion of older people in the population is increasingly creating problems. Not only is there more strain on the social system, both in public assistance and health care costs, but there is also a shrinking labor market, which can reduce a country's competitiveness in a global economy.

According to the UN, this does not lead inevitably to macroeconomic decline. Their report provides a list of things that can support an aging population *and* build economic growth, including: increase both continuing and life-long education; provide healthcare for all; encourage savings behavior and healthy lifestyles at all ages; promote employment among women, older people, and others traditionally excluded from the labor force, *coupled with a gradual increase in the official retirement age.* [The emphasis is mine.]

These are all great things to implement, but that last part is the key, and something you need to prepare yourself for. To continue to support programs like Social Security, the U.S. and other countries will push back the age at which you can start claiming benefits. That's why supporting employment beyond age 65 is so important. And that's why health and wellness program are so critical to keeping healthcare costs down.

China, which has among the lowest ages for starting retirement (from age 50 for blue-collar women up to age 60 for most men), is in a particularly thorny place as it tries to adjust its public assistance policies. But how best to support an aging population is something every country needs to give serious attention to.

Unless you're living in a place like Okinawa, where they don't even have a word for "retirement." People there just work until they can't work any longer, which is actually the way it was throughout the world until the late 1800s.

> **Takeaway #4:** The more you can rely on your own plans and how you support your later years, the less likely you are to be disrupted by policy changes from the government. As well, the more you can maintain your health, the less impact you'll have on both your own finances and those of the country.

Language

For something as special as retirement is held up to be, you'd think there would be a snappier way to talk about it. Something like "Ultimate Freedom" or "Play Time" or maybe even "Woohoo, I Made It!" for those who envision a release from work and a 30-year vacation.

Can you imagine that conversation?

"Hey, Carl, long time no see. Are you woohooed now?"

"Not yet, Jerry, but I CAN.NOT.WAIT."

Instead of calling them "retirees," we could call them "woohoos." That would spice up news reports, like "A group of woohoos was caught skinny dipping in Barnard Lake last night."

I guess "retirement" is what we get for relying on droll politicians to lead the way. Del Webb's marketing machine came up with a beauty in "Your Golden Years," but by then, the word "retirement" was the standard way to describe this time in one's life.

There's nothing sunny or uplifting about the word, however. Here's a selection of synonyms: give up; withdraw; retreat; depart; give way; loneliness; surrender; abdicate; resignation; exit; end. Those make you feel all bouncy and limitless, don't they? There is also "leisure," but it's the only one that doesn't have a shroud around it, and there are no synonyms that scream "Paaaaarrrrtttyyy," which is how some people (usually before they retire) imagine it to be.

You may think I'm just playing around with words and it really doesn't matter, but it does. The meaning of words affect your thoughts, which affect your feelings, your actions, and your results. Many people have made a distinction in their minds between the meaning of the word and how they want to picture it, but that meaning lurks there even with the sunniest of plans and expectations. We'll talk more in the next chapter about the impact of words and what neuroscience recommends we do.

The thing is, even though I would love for us to retire the word "retirement" (and banish "retiree" along with it), I don't have a good replacement for it; somehow, "Not Working" falls flat. The Brits use the word "Pensioners" and other European languages have a variation on that, but none of these sound particularly inspiring.

The Spanish have something with potential. They call this time in one's life "jubilación" which looks just like "jubilation" in English. (The translation actually is "retirement.") Now, "jubilación" sounds bright and engaging, but when I asked a friend who's lived in Spain for 25 years if everyone there is jubilant in their later years, she said, "No." In fact, while English is her mother tongue, she hadn't even made the connection between "jubilación" and "jubilation" until I mentioned it.

Even if "jubilación" was a magic word with powers to create a happy populace, the reality is that it would never be widely adopted; "retirement" and "pensioners" and the like are too deeply embedded in their respective cultures.

But how you define it for yourself matters a lot. And whether you even use the word "retirement" is up to you. If it helps to call this your Third Act, Third Age, Third Wave, or Second Half, use what serves you. Or just say something like "I'm still working" or "I'm exploring new things" — something that gives you new territory to explore with a conversation partner. If you just say, "I'm retired," you're likely to be pigeonholed as someone who has nothing more to offer to life. And that sucks for everybody.

Takeaway #5: We're stuck with the word "retirement" and it's variations ("retired," "retiree," et al). But nothing obligates you to use any of those. So resist the temptation to say, now or in the future, "I'm retired." There are so many more engaging and uplifting ways to describe yourself.

Stages of Retirement

A lot of people think of retirement like it's a finish line, like once they reach it, they've achieved their goal — or partial goal, if they're "partially retired" — and now everything is set for them. But it's not a finish line, it's just an inflection point, and you've got so many years left to do something constructive, fun, and engaging, or to get swallowed by fear, uncertainty, and doubt about what to do and what the future holds.

If you delve into retirement-focused articles or books, you're bound to come across descriptions of the phases of retirement. Depending on which piece you read, there could be three phases or as many as seven. Ultimately, they're all talking about the same thing, and they often come to the same conclusion about the key to a happy retirement. Let's break all this down.

At it's simplest, we've got Before Retirement and In Retirement ("After Retirement" is another matter altogether). Some people divide up the Before phase into periods of time, like "five years before" and "one year before". This is a phase of planning, anticipation, and probably the occasional freakout.

Next up are the early days of retirement, typically the first year or two; several writers have referred to this as the "honeymoon" phase. This is where you check things off your to-do lists and your bucket list.

But around two to three years in, there begins the "disenchantment" phase, where the plans you made don't seem as compelling, or you've worked through all your lists and are lost trying to figure out what's next. One pair of writers calls this "Retirement Hell."

Next is a phase where you develop new ideas about your future and maybe even about who you are in this world. "Reorientation" is the most common word used for this phase.

Finally, there is the "Reconciliation" phase, which is typically pegged at about 15 years into retirement. This is where things seem to be set and settled in your life, where everything seems to flow.

The important thing is not how many phases there are, but that there *are* phases and you will go through them. Almost no one has a straight line from "I'm retiring today" to "I've been happy to my last breath."

How much time you spend in each of these phases will be unique to you. You might fly through some or get stuck and keep recycling a particular phase. Eventually, most people get through them all.

As for the common answer on how best to navigate these phases, it's in having a purpose that pulls you forward and inspires you to get into action every day.

Takeaway #6: There is no finish line once you retire. It's just the next day, waiting to be lived. How you handle that transition into retirement and all the phases awaiting you will determine how well your retirement goes.

Summary

- Plan your transition when it makes sense for you, not according to your age. There's nothing magical about 65.

- Don't be seduced by marketing images and messages about how retirement is supposed to be. They're just trying to sell you stuff. Paint your own picture of what it can and should be. Few people have that all-sunny, all-the-time life anyway.

- The more self-reliant you can be in funding your retirement, the better. The rules about Social Security, Medicare, and other programs *will* change.

▪ As much as you can, use words other than "retirement" to describe this new time in your life. It's far better to talk about what you're up to, rather than to label yourself in a way that's easy to dismiss.

▪ Accept that retirement will not be smooth sailing to your final day, and that there are distinct phases you'll go through before everything truly flows.

What are your biggest takeaways from this chapter?

When Do You Become Old?

It is not old age that is at fault,
but rather our attitudes towards it.
· Cicero (1st century BC) ·

"Anyone in their mid-to-late 30s have frequent, quiet, but total freak outs about how old you are? Like absolute existential melt downs?"

That was a post on Twitter by a hero of mine, Casey Neistat, as he neared the perilous age of 40. It wasn't a new phenomenon for him; there's a video clip of him at 35 saying he's old. This particular tweet got nearly seven hundred replies, some of which said being older is no big deal. Most responses, however, were in lockstep with Casey, moaning about mortality sinking in. Some respondents said they'd been freaking out about their age since their 20s.

A few weeks later, after turning 40, Casey continued on his theme of being old. In response to someone else's tweet about how our speed as runners declines as we age, with a graph that showed speeds starting to drop around age 40, Casey declared this to be "conclusive, irrefutable evidence that when you turn 40 you are indeed old."

Boy, he's going to have a long time to be old.

There is no absolute number that defines when you're old or not; there's no demarcation, at the stroke of some midnight, that proclaims you are now a different person than you were one minute before. And yet the idea is something you can probably understand, if not in fact identify with. "Milestone birthdays" are often greeted with more dread than delight, as if turning 30, 40, 50, or older is just the latest sign of losing your grip on youth and further cementing your place in the Land of Irrelevancy.

What we're witnessing here is ageism, but directed at one's self. That may seem bizarre, that people would *choose* to think less of themselves and *choose* to limit their possibilities for the future. But when you've been programmed almost since birth to hold older people in low regard, to ignore and reject them, you can see why Casey and others would freak out about joining a club they don't want to be part of. It suggests that their life will have less meaning or impact, and that they will increasingly be left out of opportunities and, really, left out of life.

That's not to say that everyone discriminates against older people. In some cultures and some families, older people are revered. They are the holders of wisdom and experience and patience and love. But I wasn't raised that way and chances are most readers of this book weren't raised that way either.

It Starts When We're Young

What we learn when we're very young tends to stick with us and define our thoughts and attitudes throughout our life. These neural pathways are laid down through repetitions of images and experiences, helping children learn how the world works and their place in it. One of the most influential sources for developing young children's values, beliefs, and behaviors is books, particularly books with lots of illustrations. These create a sense of what life is like, what belongs, and what is important.

I'm sure no creator of these books set out to specifically stick it to older people, but they did, certainly up to the 1990s. If older people were shown at all, which was rare, they were typically depicted as dull, drab, frail, and sad. Their roles were mostly inconsequential, and the way they were drawn ticked all the stereotypes: stooped over; wearing ill-fitting clothes; often with a cane, a walker, or a rocking chair. The ladies had their hair in a bun, the men had mustaches, and everyone wore glasses. Or, if they had some flair and fire in them, they were the evil forces trying to stop the young hero.

Kids are wonderful little sponges and have picked up on these impressions, because these images have been presented and reinforced to them as what is normal. Some studies suggest that children as young as three hold negative ideals of older adults, and these impressions are expanded as they reach school age, both because there haven't been, until recently, depictions to counteract those early ones, and because children are exposed to a wider variety of media that continue to promote the idea that older people are "dirtier, uglier, less healthy, and less helpful than younger adults," according to one research study. Just think about the line, "Get off my lawn!" What comes to mind? And when did this impression get planted in your brain?

A more recent, and horrible, example of ageist programming for kids has been popping up in elementary schools across America. To celebrate reaching 100 days of class, and to help young kids grasp the value of 100 as a quantity, some schools are staging a "Dress Up As A 100 Year-Old Person" day. With glee, parents are dressing up their kids to look "old," as they imagine it to be — dumpy, frumpy, baggy clothes, white hair, lots of wrinkles, stooped postures, walkers and canes, slow movements, shaky voices, and so on. The more outrageous the better, as one blogger wrote. And in asking kids to act out these stereotypes, parents and teachers are cementing the idea that older people are a singular class that can be mocked and dismissed as easily as wiping off the sketched-on wrinkles. Among the gushing comments by one person, regarding a photo of a boy heavily made-up and leaning on a cane, "He looks like he loves a good early-bird special."

Things are improving in children's literature and media depictions, with more accurate and uplifting portrayals of older people. Two great examples are the Pixar films "Up" and "Coco," which feature older people in realistic and positive ways. They also show intergenerational relationships that are wonderful models for young kids to see.

If you were born in the 1980s or earlier, however, you've already metabolized those highly discriminatory impressions about older people. As researcher Phyllis Barnum noted in 1977: "[Children's] literature helps educate young children to the belief that old people are unimportant and that old age is not an enjoyable time of life."

Age 30? Let the Freak Outs Begin

When you read about women in their 20s getting Botox injections ("Just to soften my lines..."), or men in their 30s, particularly in the tech world, getting plastic surgery to look younger and thus improve their employment chances, you can see how early and powerfully these toxic beliefs impact people's lives.

People are freaked out about getting older, becoming irrelevant, or feeling past their prime. Ours is a youth-obsessed culture and older people just don't fit into that narrative. So with each new wrinkle and each white strand of hair, the desperation rises. No wonder, in 2015 alone, more than $114 billion were spent on products and services to try to keep aging at bay.

For decades, older people in ad campaigns came in two flavors. Either they looked like prototypical retirees, as the background for medical device and pharmaceutical ads, or they were glamorized to sell upscale products. I realize a lumpy-looking older guy probably wouldn't sell as many designer jeans as a trim, tanned, aging Adonis, but the obsession with looks has just shifted the age markers, not erased them, and the idealized form of youth, slim and sinewy, remains — just in a time-burnished form.

Examples of a glorious life in one's later years, or even just a simple, happy life, have only recently made it into the conversation. Some advertisers are realizing they'll sell more if they show "real" older people, not just the 22% who are looking for a "golden years" retirement. Or Instagram accounts like @Gramparents and the wonderful new podcast, *70 over 70*, which is focused on "How do we make the most of the time we have left?" Netflix has given us series like *Grace and Frankie* and *The Kominsky Method* that show more accurate depictions of life as older adults. And we're getting more realistic films with older actors as lead characters facing real problems, not just wacky-older-neighbor-does-weird-shit.

But in our daily lives, whether out on the street, in a store, on a bus or a beach, we tend to see what we expect, which is — if older people are there at all — they look sad and worn and out of place. And all this reaffirms the lessons we first learned in children's books: old age is not an enjoyable time of life.

For many people, this rejection of being old continues even into their later years. You might think that once someone is officially a part of this older cohort, at whatever age that happens, they would embrace their new tribe. But several researchers have found that not only do older people perceive themselves to be younger than they are, but they also tend to reject others of a similar age or older, because they don't want to be associated with that caste. It's the perfect embodiment of Groucho Marx's famous line, "I wouldn't want to belong to any group that would have me as a member."

And so the wheel of ageism takes another turn.

Where Ageism Lurks

Ageism is considered to be the last socially acceptable prejudice and you see its influence everywhere. It shows up in obvious ways, like when people are turned down for jobs because they're presumed to no longer have the mental or physical capacity to do the job. Or when companies push out older workers whom they fear will be off the job more frequently due to health reasons, driving up health care costs. Or it's presumed that they're too expensive to hire, or they can't work with younger bosses or coworkers. Or they're considered irrelevant because they've been around too long, or they don't fit the culture, or that they shouldn't wear what they want because it doesn't look good on old bodies, or — well, you get the picture. I know from personal experience how much it sucks to be dismissed purely because of your age.

There are also less obvious ways that ageism creeps in, and they're just as pernicious. Take a phrase like, "He's 80 years *young!*" That may sound like a compliment, but it's not. It still makes a distinction between being old and being young, with young as the ideal. Or in a story about a 107-year old woman testifying before Congress, she was described as "speaking in a strong, clear voice." Would anyone say that about a 40-year old? Of course not.

Or "You look great for your age!" Well, how did you imagine they should look? Wretched and decrepit? Even "Senior Discounts" turn older people into a special class that allegedly deserves attention. But make no mistake about this, those discounts are just a marketing ploy to get older people to shop there.

These kinds of words and actions, even if well-intended, serve to remind older people — and those who will become older people — that they are different and in need of special treatment. And that can batter people's self-image and their health, even if they're not conscious of it.

Lots of research studies have established the damaging effects of negative self-perceptions that are experienced by older individuals. These impacts include increases in blood pressure, diabetes, and obesity, as well as social isolation and depression. By contrast, a positive self-perception lowers the markers for these and other diseases and helps extend not only one's quality of life, but also their life span. In fact, Becca Levy at Yale found that study participants with more positive self-perceptions of aging lived an average of **7.5 years longer** than those with more negative self-perceptions of aging.

Can you imagine that? Getting seven or more years of life to enjoy, likely in better health, just by changing your mindset? I'm still blown away by this statistic. What could you do with an extra 7.5 years?

Resisting these negative stereotypes, however, is hard. They're so pervasive! How do you shut out the barrage from ads, movies and TV, books, clothing design, industrial design, health care services, social services, and, particularly, just casual conversations with friends and family that all say being young is better, and being old is bad. It's insidious how people toss off words and phrases that actually have negative aging connotations.

This happens, as well, in our own heads. Here's something I had to catch myself on recently. I was lifting weights at the gym and saw a guy, seemingly older than me, with spindly legs and a kind of crooked stance. Because I'm still fighting this impulse to judge people that was planted deep in my brain at an early age, my first thought was that he'd probably do a few light weights and then walk off. Boy, was I wrong. This guy was a beast. On the leg press machine, he pushed far more weight than I ever have. He lifted more weight than I typically do. And when he got on a treadmill, he practically flew. I was stunned, and pleased for him — and ashamed at how I'd first reacted. I am making conscious efforts to not repeat such a stupid reaction.

But my programming, and yours, and everyone else's isn't something we can resolve with a snap of our fingers. It takes awareness, it takes repetition of new behaviors like I'm doing, and it takes vigilance to not be sucked back into those damaging ways of thinking so many of us learned.

As for the bigger fight against ageism, there are some people who are tackling it head on, from Ashton Applewhite, who wrote a stirring anti-ageist manifesto, *This Chair Rocks,* to Ken Dychtwald who has been on this beat for over thirty years and written numerous books on the subject, to Marc Middleton and his team at Growing Bolder, which is bringing a fresh, personal, media-savvy approach to showing how positive-aging can be achieved, and Chip Conley, who wrote a book called *Wisdom@Work* and has established the Modern Elder Academy to help people redefine themselves in the next chapter of their lives. There are many more people I could highlight here; look for an expanded list in the Resources section of this book.

The thing is, for all the recent focus on wiping out ageism, it's barely changed. In the 1600s, Cotton Mather, a fiery preacher who was a big promoter of witch trials, said about older people, "Be so wise as to disappear of your own accord." Now fast forward to 2020, when celebrated comedian Patton Oswalt, upon turning 50, said of Baby Boomers, "You've got to get the fuck out of the way . . . Have some grace. Bow out gracefully."

And all those suggestions, as the Covid-19 pandemic threatened to overwhelm hospitals, that in the event of a shortage of ventilators, older people should be sacrificed if a younger person was also in need of such life support. That's not an easy decision to make, but to take down a whole population of people just because of their age? That's just wrong.

Yes, ageism is still very much alive. The question then is what do you want to do about it?

What Can You Do About Ageism?

If you search the web on "how to beat ageism," almost every article is about how to try to counteract it in job searches. Many posts, in fact, focus just on how to reformat your resume to try to defuse ageist reactions. But does that shift the tide on ageism? Not at all. Even if you're clever with your resume, very often when a hiring manager sees you, any gray hairs or wrinkles may lower your chances dramatically.

The damaging effects of ageism go way beyond just workplace issues. So how do you deal with that — with discriminations that transcend the workplace, with the cutting words and rejections and self-sabotage because someone is considered "old?"

A better model for attacking this is to look at how people are trying to turn the tide on racism. And the pattern is pretty simple, even if enacting it is hard. It's about Awareness, Integration, and Activism.

It starts with you. With your attitudes about getting older, your thoughts about others who are aging, and any feelings about roles and behaviors for older people, both in the workplace and in society. Test your awareness of how you might be contributing to the idea that older people are somehow less than fully capable individuals worthy of respect and opportunity.

As you develop your awareness, pay attention to the words you use to describe older people. If you use terms like "the elderly," "seniors," "senior moment," "golden years," or worse ("geezers," "hags," etc.), those aren't funny and they're not harmless. Your words and the ideas behind them put a distance between you and others — and they put a distance between yourself now and how you will be in the future when you are old enough to perhaps be stereotyped these ways.

After tuning into your own ageist tendencies and beginning to overcome them, the next step is to find opportunities to interact with people older than yourself. Lots of studies have been done on the impact of intergenerational interactions, and the signs are really encouraging. When we spend time with others — of any age, racial background, identity, and such — we come away with new, positive perspectives on them, their experiences, and their dreams. Put more simply, when we get to know others, we no longer see them as objects or categories; we see them as people. And when we invite older people into our world, not only do ageist barriers start to fall away, but we gain new perspectives on a life we're headed toward. At the same time, the people you interact with get a chance to be seen and understood for who they are, and that's a priceless gift.

These interactions could be as simple as saying hello on the street. Or asking about their day. Or you could go all in and volunteer at some activity where older people might be. That could be at an assisted living facility, but it could also be at, say, a road race — if you pay attention, you'll find lots of older participants who you might previously have overlooked. Just look around and then take the first step to interact.

The final step, when you're ready for it, is to actively work to end ageism. Whether we can do that in our lifetime is doubtful, but we can make a dent in it, and with enough dents from enough people around the world, we *can* change the tide of ageism.

The prescription above is just a starting point. There is a wonderful resource started by Ashton Applewhite called Old School; you can find it at OldSchool.info. This is a clearinghouse for all things against ageism: tools; books; blogs and papers; campaigns; speakers; videos; organizations; and podcasts. If someone is doing something to combat ageism, perhaps even in your community, you're likely to find it at Old School. She also has a thought-provoking site called, "Yo, Is This Ageist?" (yoisthisageist.com), where she deconstructs queries and items that readers send in. If you're curious about whether something is ageist, be sure to click the "Ask" tab.

I hope you've got a new perspective now on just how pervasive is ageism, and perhaps have some ideas of how to combat it. If you're going to have a successful retirement, or non-retirement, you can't be an ostrich about ageism. But taking these steps, even if you're rallying on the battlements of anti-ageist campaigns, doesn't ensure that you will be magically cured of all those ageist thoughts and behaviors that have perniciously picked away at your self-esteem and your plans for the future. So how do you turn around your thoughts about *yourself*? Let's dig into that.

So When Do You Become "Old?"

Have you picked out a specific date, like my hero Casey who declared that when he turned 40 he was officially old? Maybe it's when you get your first letter inviting you to join AARP? Or when you qualify for "Senior Discounts" or Medicare?

Or do you have a vague sense it's coming and you're dreading it, until the day you turn around and say, "Holy fuck, I'm OLD now?"

That vagueness is the worst, because it will just silently pick at you and your sense of what's possible as you get older. If you've heard the phrase, "Death by a thousand cuts," this is exactly that scenario.

Let's get to something concrete instead. That will give you more control over what's happening in your head and your heart. And if your selected date for being old is far enough away, you'll have lots of time to forget about it because, well, you're not there yet.

So pick a date, or at least an age. And remember there's nothing magical about 65 as the marker of being old; that was chosen by many different groups for economic reasons.

If you're struggling to figure out a specific date, ask yourself what's your definition of old. Is it when someone seems to be forgetful all the time? Maybe they seem mentally incompetent? Or they're experiencing physical declines? Slowed capabilities?

As you ponder those, please realize that many people live to their hundreds without experiencing any of those things (other than seeing their 10k race times get longer). These are not guaranteed afflictions or experiences that everyone has as they age.

Here's an exercise to try — you're going to interview your older self. Pick an age at which you're sure you'll be old and then, like an actor, try to "be" that age, both mentally and physically. You might want to have paper and a pen nearby to record your answers. Ready?

Hi there, old person. Tell us . . .
- What's the impact of being old?
- What did you have to stop or give up? (Sports? Sex? Solid food?)
- How are you now "less than" or deficient?
- Will you always stay this way or get even older than "old?"
- What if you got less old?
- What would be the impact of that?
- What do you fear about being old?

If you really went through that list and effectively lived the experience of being old, what's your perspective now? Do you have a clearer sense of when you'll officially be old, or are you tired of thinking about this and want to move on?

The reality is there's no proof that any specific age is definitively old. Sure, people in their 80s and beyond, or even in their 60s, show some degree of the effects of aging on their bodies, but none of that categorically defines them as old. And while others may say otherwise, perhaps even loudly, you will never be old until YOU decide that you are. And if you never buy into being old, no matter what may be going on with your body or mind, then you *won't* be old.

There's a lovely story of 106-year old dancer Eileen Kramer from Sydney, who is still performing regularly and refuses to use the word "old." According to Eileen, "I'm not old, I've just been here a long time and learned a few things along the way."

Life At A Crossroads

My hero, Casey Neistat, has an important role in this story, one which may hit home with you. But before we get into why he's so relevant here, it's useful to understand why he matters to me.

I never had a hero growing up, not even my dad. It wasn't until my 20s, when I was an actor in New York, that I finally landed on a hero: Charlie Chaplin. His creativity was staggering and the breadth of his work — from actor to director to screenwriter, set designer, composer, lyricist, and producer — was and is unheard of. He was bold, funny, surprising, and his films were incredibly moving. I couldn't get enough of him. And while I had no aspirations to do all that he did, a part of me wanted to be like him.

A few more heroes popped up during my acting years: Dustin Hoffman; Meryl Streep; Derek Jacobi. All of them so varied and wonderful in what they did. And in the writing world, I've been entranced with Elmore Leonard, Christopher Moore, and Jen Sincero. Each in their realm have been bold, surprising, funny, and deep.

Then YouTube hit my radar, as I was thinking about how to promote my business. I can't remember where or when I first heard about Casey, but once I saw one of his videos, I was hooked. He looks kind of quirky and there's a raw quality to his videos (though they are masterfully edited), but that's all part of the attraction. He is as real as real gets.

Casey's videos walk the same heroes' path for me — bold, funny, surprising, personal — with an added layer of not giving a fuck about what others say. His manifesto for reinventing yourself is his film "Do What You Can't." (Co-created with Max Joseph; it's easy to find this on YouTube.) It is a rallying cry for pursuing what you want in life, without being held back by anyone's expectations, including your own.

"Do What You Can't" opens with Casey dressed in a tuxedo and dangling fifteen feet below a helicopter as it flies above Los Angeles. His voiceover starts with "To the haters, the doubters, my 7th-grade vice principal. To everyone who's ever told anyone with a dream they can't — this video is for you." He then goes on to obliterate the idea that you might have limits on what you can do. It is outrageously original, bold, funny, and stirring. When I need a shot of adrenaline for my creativity, I watch this video. I have no desire to dangle below a helicopter, but that unrestrained joy and off-the-wall creativity is a touchstone for my video efforts.

Once, Nike hired him to create a video for its new FuelBand exercise tracker, with a tag line of "Make It Count." Nike thought they would get a product video from a guy with millions of followers. But Casey and Max decided instead to use Nike's money to travel the world and keep going until the funds ran out; it took ten days. Nike was pissed at first, but the video has had over 31 million views and was incredibly successful in supporting Nike's goals. Casey and Max showed what it really means to make something count.

Casey created and posted a new video for 500 consecutive days, across a dizzying array of topics, because he felt so compelled. He is a legend in the YouTube creator community.

So tell me, how can a guy that bold and creative roll up in a ball of "old" and shrink from life? He posted once about wanting, in his "old man years," to be like these older Italian gentlemen, called Umarells, who stand around all day at construction sites just watching the work being done. Clearly, he has a deeply ingrained belief that when you're old, all you can do is watch life go by.

What makes this even more perplexing is that he did a video honoring his grandmother, a former Radio City Music Hall Rockette, who was still teaching tap dancing and staging recitals into her 90s. She certainly wasn't slowing down.

I would bet money, however, that once Casey gets past the "poor me" phase of being older, his creativity will kick in big time. Maybe it will be with more videos or maybe it will be with something completely different, but his is a spirit that can't stay hidden for long. He didn't have a cushy life growing up, and the driving force that elevated him from high school dropout and teenage father to millionaire media star is just waiting to kick in again.

And Casey will continue to personify what I fully believe: you are never out of the game.

From Humble Beginnings

To drive home this last point, here are stories of two women who didn't let age or experiences keep them from trying new things, and breaking significant records.

Lynn Salvo was approaching her 50th birthday. Wife, mother, teacher, and self-described as pudgy, she began to feel like it was time to make some changes in her life. "I did not want to be fifty like '50' means to some people," she said in an interview. So she took up running — and was initially wiped out after a short distance. But within six weeks, she was up to five miles at a time.

Four years later, she was running so much and so well that she qualified for and ran the Boston Marathon. She moved on to triathlons for six years, and then just cycling for another five years. All this time, she was still teaching.

After she retired in 2014, things got interesting. She joined a cycling club, started riding 300 miles a week, and did her first cross-country trip with friends. She was hooked.

In 2016, at age 66, she set a Guinness World Record as the oldest woman to cross the United States by bicycle — 3163 miles in 59 days. Her mantra during that time was a quote by Eleanor Roosevelt, "Do the thing you think you cannot do." (That sounds familiar…)

The next year, she set another Guinness World Record, this time as the oldest woman to cross Canada by bike. She was planning to ride through Europe, from top to bottom, nearly 5000 miles, until it was postponed due to the pandemic.

What an inspiration she is. And she's all the more remarkable because of how inauspicious were her goals on the cusp of her 50th birthday. She just wanted to get fit and change her routine; she wasn't planning to set Guinness World Records. But something seized her along the way and the rest truly is history.

Rebecca Rusch didn't seem bound for greatness as a kid, not having shown any kind of athletic prowess when she was younger. She only joined the cross-country team in high school because she wanted to get the cool track suit, and she was concerned about gaining weight. She thrived in that environment, being part of a team and learning to push herself physically and mentally, and she even made all-state in one of her disciplines. But she quit her college running team her first year because the coach was a jerk, and she just got on with life.

In her mid-20s, she was working at a health club that had a climbing wall and she was captivated by that. She started climbing, got better at it, and eventually was not just teaching climbing, but also doing big wall climbs in Yosemite and Zion National Parks. She holds several female first-ascents.

With all that upper body strength, she was invited to join an elite outrigger canoe team, despite having a big fear of water. That led to being recruited to a U.S. Women's white water rafting team. And her combo of paddling skills, climbing skills, and running background made her an attractive candidate for joining a multi-day adventure racing team. For each of these sports, she was initially hesitant about getting involved, but she swallowed her fears and ultimately achieved great success. In adventure racing, she was a member of championship teams in the toughest races on the planet. She did that for several years, until there were two fatalities in the same year, and that wiped out her passion for the sport.

Later that year, her biggest sponsor ended their contract with Rebecca's team, due to a corporate buyout. At age 38, she was left wondering what she would do with her life. She'd had an incredible career so far. Maybe it was time to hang things up? That was the advice of many people around her.

Her one remaining sponsor, Red Bull, said, "You have a year left on your contract. Go do something amazing!" Their support was liberating, but Rebecca had no idea what she might do.

A friend suggested she get into endurance mountain bike racing. She could certainly handle 24-hour races physically, but she hated mountain biking and felt she had no technique. While she had to ride mountain bikes in her adventure races, those were the parts she always dreaded. To do that sport exclusively? She was not convinced.

Eventually she came around to the idea, won some big races right away, improved her bike skills, and ultimately became one of the most successful mountain bikers in history. In 2019, she was named to the Mountain Bike Hall of Fame. She holds seven world championship titles, and won the Leadville Trail 100, the most prestigious mountain bike race in America, four years in a row. She then branched out, becoming the first person to ride the 1200-mile length of the Ho Chi Minh Trail in Vietnam, and winning an Emmy for the documentary of her adventure. She's also twice won the bike division of the 350-mile Iditarod Trail invitational in Alaska in the self-supported category. Her list of accomplishments is astounding.

I knew none of this when I saw a CNN report about "The Queen of Pain." (She was labeled that by Adventure Sports Magazine, both for what she could endure and what she inflicted on her competitors.) What stuck with me from that CNN profile and led me to study her life were her words at the end of the piece.

"I'm 52 now. Being an ultra-endurance athlete, it's my life. I've been doing it for decades and I can't imagine separating it. People ask me 'When are you going to retire? When are you going to stop doing this?' The answer is 'Never' because this is actually part of who I am."

Remember, you are only "old" if you tell yourself you are. I invite you to never use that word again, about yourself or others.

What are your biggest takeaways from this chapter?

"Oh, Shit!" Moments in Aging

"Am I WHAT?"

"Are you retired?" my friend said again.

That question caught me by surprise.

It wasn't unreasonable to ask. I hadn't seen Jack in years and retirement was very much on *his* mind, since he was within months of wrapping up a 30-year career. We're close in age, so he probably thought that if he was retiring, I might be too.

But I hadn't spent years looking forward to the day when I didn't have to work any longer. I love having something big and juicy on which to focus my creativity and passion, so the thought of just stopping all that and going on a 30-year vacation has held no allure.

My read on retirement might've been different if I had stayed in one line of work for 30 years. Maybe I would've gotten bored or tired of the process after all that time, and thus would've embraced a Free-me-from-this-existence! attitude about retirement. As it is, I'm on my sixth career and loving it.

To be fair, I had probably been asked that question many times before; it had just never landed so sharply. And that's the thing with both ageist hits and the various signs that we're getting older — they often arrive like Carl Sandberg's "Fog," stalking in on little cat feet to go unnoticed or to seem like they'd been there all along. These reminders of the march of time, whether damning or benign, provide opportunities for us to either sink from the weight of our inexorable decline, or to say, "Hell, no! I'm not done yet."

One of the key ways we learn new things and make discoveries about ourselves is through the experiences of others. So to help you grapple with aging, I offer my growing collection of "Oh, Shit!" moments — those occasions when I was starkly reminded that I'm getting older and that some things can't be reversed. Individually, they may not seem like much, but taken as a complete set, they mark an important part of my progression through life. They also affect how I assess my prospects for the future. See how many of these sound familiar.

AGE 32: Discovering during orientation for the MBA program at UCLA that I was one of the oldest members of the in-coming class. I still remember the side glances I got, but it was quickly a non-issue.

AGE 34: Hearing that an advertising agency wouldn't hire me because they thought I wouldn't be able to work for a boss who was younger than me. This was before such overt ageism was outlawed.

AGE 42: Realizing I needed bifocal lenses and reading glasses. Also, as a new parent, that I would be 60 before my first child graduated from high school.

AGE 40-ish: Getting basal cell carcinomas (the "good kind of cancer," as my first dermatologist said) and colon polyps. Those aren't strictly a sign of aging, but they can come as you add years to your life.

AGE 45: Dealing with my wife's presumption, as I began job hunting after three years as a stay-at-home-dad, that no one would hire me because of my age. I got a job pretty quickly and ended up as VP of Marketing for a successful Silicon Valley startup.

AGE 50: Receiving my first "Join us!" mailer from AARP. Despite all the discounts that members get, I didn't sign up until 15 years later.

AGE 59: Learning that my brother-in-law, who's a few years younger than me, was taking blood pressure meds. I'd thought those were just for older people. Fast forward eight years and I started taking those, too.

AGE 60: Discovering that I've SHRUNK! WTF?! Somehow, I'd lost two inches off my height. That was a depressing moment. I thought this happened much later in life.

AGE 61: Hearing my mom say, "Where's your blood pressure monitor?" when she came to visit. Was I supposed to have one, like having a fire extinguisher in your home? (I have one now, for me, not just for guests.)

AGE 62: Listening to my wife extol the virtues of being a bus driver, since that was the only job she thought I could get at my age after I shut down my software business.

AGE 63: Being horribly patronized by a 30-something woman about my assumed lack of technical skills, while I was running lighting and sound for an improv comedy club. It turned out she knew far less about technology than I did.

AGE 65: Signing up for Medicare. That was actually a good thing, since it's more affordable than self-insuring, but I needed to sign up with AARP to get a better rate on a supplemental plan. If not a negative, it wasn't a moment for celebration.

Here's a collection of other "Oh, Shit!" moments for which I don't have a date stamp.

- Rectal exams. Thinning hair. Sagging eye lids. Jowls.

- Finding out I'm in the early stages of macular degeneration, and needing to add yet another pill to my daily collection. I'm up to six pills now — a blood thinner, one for cholesterol, one for blood pressure, Vitamin D, Vitamin B-12, and the eye pill — and I will have to take most, if not all, for the rest of my days.

■ Realizing my teeth are shifting, despite all that painful and expensive orthodontia long ago.

■ Being struck by tinnitus (ears) and floaters (eyes) ON THE SAME DAY! These are afflictions from which there is no escape.

■ Getting asked — in medical offices, at the hair cutters, and in random conversations — if I'm retired. It's such a knee-jerk question. And being grilled by medical professionals as to whether I've fallen recently. Yikes!

■ Needing progressively more dental work, including root canals, crowns, and just random replacements of decades-old fillings. It's numbing. (pardon the pun ;)

■ Having osteoarthritis in my right knee, which has killed my ability to ski, run, and, surprisingly, to ride a bike pain-free. I met with a doctor who said part of my knee was shot, but the overall structure was good and he wouldn't do a knee replacement.

■ Realizing it takes me longer to recover from a 5-mile hike in the hills, and that I'm slower than I was ten years ago. Worse, I'm slower in the pool than I was 30 years ago. That's to be expected, but part of me believes I should still be able to swim like I did before.

I think that's the whole catalog. The thing is, despite this great mass of maladies and BS I shoulder every day, they don't define who I am. Not one of these, let alone the entire collection, is a sign that I am "old" — they're just signs that I'm getting older. Some I bear with grace, some (especially the ageist ones) piss me off, and some, like the end of skiing and running, make me a little sad.

But I'm here. I'm alive. I've been given the gift of more than 25,000 days on this planet and, God willing, will have at least another 10,000 days. This is a cause for celebration and gratitude, not despair. When so many people don't even get this many days, how can I be depressed about getting another morning, and another morning?

Does that mean my life is glorious and perfect? Not at all.

But realizing that I've probably passed the midpoint of my life, I don't want to waste any time moaning about all the things I can't do any longer. Sure, my lap times are slower, but I still get to freaking swim and that's something joyous to me.

And all the things I'm launching, and all the things yet to come that at this moment I have no idea are awaiting me — those are frickin' miracles and something to race toward, not recede from, no matter how many pills I take or which aches and pains I may carry with me on the journey.

I'm still going, and I hope you are, too. Who knows what's over the next horizon?

What are some of your "Oh, Shit!" moments in aging?

Optimize Your Life

"Your calculated life expectancy is 102 years."

Whoa. That beat the target I'd long held for myself of living to 98.

This proclamation was from a very extensive online quiz I took recently. There are lots of life expectancy calculators out there, but most of them are limited in scope. This one had 40 questions, some for which I had to dig to find answers (Where were those blood test results anyway?). This quiz by Dr. Thomas Perls seems to be the pinnacle for such quizzes; you'll find a link in the Resources chapter.

There's no guarantee that I'll live that long. But considering what I have working against me — family history of heart issues, three bouts already with atrial fibrillation, weight issues, etc — I was surprised it was that high. Of course, I do have a stellar diet, I gave up alcohol, I exercise most days, I never smoked, and my mind is set on living a long time in good health, so those definitely helped my score.

But still, 102? Since I'm 68 as I write this, that gives me 34 more years to live. That's a long time! So the question then is "How do I want to live those years?" Quick answer: happy; healthy; connected; engaged; inspired every day. To achieve that, I need to do everything I can to boost my health and fitness, care for my body and mind, and keep my attitude high about life and my future.

Surprisingly, there is no such thing as dying of old age. From a study of more than 42,000 autopsies, centenarians (people who've lived to 100) died of a disease or illness in every instance; none of them died of "old age."

Genetics play a part in how long you live, but scientists believe that 75-80% of your longevity is dependent on epigenetics or "lifestyle factors" — things like diet, exercise, stress management, sleep, mindset, and more that you can control.

Let that sink in. The most important factors in living a long, healthy, fruitful life *are in your control.* That doesn't mean you are guaranteed to make it to 100 just by eating a kale salad with chia seeds sprinkled over it every day. But when you can choose to do things that increase your chances of living longer and healthier, and that are likely to save you both money and suffering, why wouldn't you? Making these choices isn't just an insurance policy against things like dementia and heart disease; what you'll find below can increase your resilience, your strength, and your enjoyment of life. [*Note: before making significant changes in your diet or starting an exercise program, check with your doctor.*]

In my research, across books, articles, and podcasts, I ended up with 32 different lists on how to live a long, healthy, happy life. The number of steps, habits, or tips they offered ranged from three things to 60. While each list had a particular theme, there were a lot of common threads. There wasn't one specific list, however, that I felt answered *everything* that you should pay attention to.

Okay, one list with 50 items did cover everything that's critical, and a lot that is helpful but not as vital. When you've got so many things vying for your attention, however, where something really important like "Purpose" is wedged between "Eat Spicy Food" and "Do Yoga," it's hard to determine what matters most.

So here is my offering — six categories, plus a chaser, with a number of critical components like diet, sleep, and strength training listed under their appropriate categories:

1. Health
2. Fitness
3. Mindset
4. Purpose
5. Social Connections
6. Finances

Now, you might think, "I've heard it all before. Get sleep. Eat your veggies. Do sudoku. Yada, yada, yada." And you will find some of that here, though perhaps with a different slant. But you're also likely to discover a few new things that could totally change your perspective. That happened for me, starting with *telomeres*.

Health

An aglet is a virtually invisible thing we rely on every day. Aglets are the plastic or metal tubes at the end of each shoelace, put there to keep your laces from unraveling. Useful? Yes. Do you need to pay attention to them? Not really, as long as they stay on and do their job.

We have something similar in our bodies that cap the ends of each strand of our DNA. These are called telomeres and, unlike aglets, we really should pay attention to them. Telomeres are not mere binding agents, they're more like defenders of the genome and protectors against cellular decay. They are so important to health and longevity that in 2009, Elizabeth Blackburn, Carol Greider, and Jack Szostak won the Nobel Prize in Medicine for their research on telomeres. Telomeres are not the only factor affecting aging, but they're a critical component.

David Sinclair in his book, *Lifespan: Why We Age — and Why We Don't Have To*, says that aging is primarily a matter of problems reading the genetic code in our cells, and epigenetic factors are key contributors in that process. So all these elements we control — diet, sleep, exercise, stress, and so on — can accelerate our deterioration OR can slow it down and perhaps even reverse the aging process. This is where telomeres come in.

As our cells divide, our DNA is copied to new cells. At the end of each of those DNA strands is a telomere, making sure that the code, basically, doesn't degrade. The more our cells divide, the shorter the telomeres get. When they become too short, they send out a signal telling the body to stop dividing those cells. Some of these cells die off, while others still do their job, but at a reduced capacity. The remaining cells are said to be senescent, and it's the accumulation of senescent cells that starts to age our body's tissues.

As our telomeres shorten, over the course of 40-60 divisions, our body starts to age and things break down. Among the resulting effects can be cancer, stroke, vascular dementia, cardiovascular disease, obesity, diabetes, and osteoporosis. But the shortening of telomeres is not a one-way march to frailty and decrepitude. Telomeres can be lengthened and lifestyle factors can keep them strong.

One intriguing study involved hyperbaric oxygen therapy (HBOT), where patients breathed pure oxygen for 90 minutes a session in a hyperbaric chamber to encourage cell growth. In this study, led by Dr. Shai Efrati, they found that HBOT can increase the length of telomeres, thereby slowing or even reversing the effects of aging.

But HBOT is seriously expensive, so we need to find other ways to try to rally our telomeres, or at least stop destroying them. Here are some science-backed approaches that can help you keep your telomeres — and your heart, your brain, and everything else — strong.

Diet

You've probably read this many times, though not with a Save The Telomeres slant: a plant-based, whole food diet is a critical component in slowing or even reversing some of the effects of aging. You'll find votes, too, for a Mediterranean diet or DASH or really anything except meat, poultry, and processed foods. According to studies cited by Dr. Michael Greger in a talk on *How Not to Die*, animal products and processed foods may cause up to 14 million deaths per year from cancer, stroke, diabetes, heart disease, and other insidious but preventable diseases.

But if you wait until you're sick to make changes to your nutrition, it will be too late. It's like deciding to give up smoking after you've been diagnosed with lung cancer; you're screwed already. So don't wait until you receive scary test results to change the course of your health and your life. Don't set yourself up to be one of those 14 million deaths each year.

Now, if juicy steaks, Chicken Saltimbocca, Fettuccini Alfredo, and mountains of fries are on the Naughty List, what can you eat? Beans, nuts, cruciferous vegetables (cauliflower, broccoli, kale, and more), other leafy green vegetables, fruits (especially berries), whole grains, spices, and more. There are countless ways to use these elements to make fabulous meals.

This book is not intended, however, to be the *F*ck Retirement Guide to Saving Your Telomeres (and Eating Healthy)*. I just wanted to put enough motivation out there to get you to look at your food choices, if they're not already super heart-mind-and-telomere healthy. You can find thousands of books devoted to this topic. There's not likely to be one single book that does it for everyone — some people like lots of facts to support their efforts and some people just want a simple plan to follow. Take this as an invitation to do some research.

As you dig into this, even if your diet is pretty exemplary, you're bound to encounter some suggestions that will be hard to, ah, swallow. Cutting back on salt? Not easy. Reducing or eliminating animal proteins? That could be rough if you've been a life-long meat eater. Restricting or even giving up on alcohol? That may be all but impossible for some people. The question is which is more important to you — continuing with the tastes, experiences, and habits you've had for years, or taking a fresh look at what you're putting in your mouth and choosing those things that will promote long-term health?

I've had an interesting journey in improving what I eat. I switched to a plant-based diet after watching the Netflix documentary, *The Game Changers*, and the transition was pretty easy, other than figuring out, "What do I eat now?" I also gave up alcohol earlier this year without much difficulty, when I found out that it can contribute to an attack of atrial fibrillation or A-Fib. I've had three bouts of A-Fib, and while none were because of alcohol, I don't want to consciously do things that I now know could spark it.

Then I learned about telomeres, and one particular thing that contributes to shorter telomeres — drinking sodas. My reaction? "Noooooooooooo!"

One of the first things I ever said was, "I want a Peppy-Cola!" (I couldn't pronounce "Pepsi" at the time.) I never became a coffee drinker, so my caffeine of choice in college was sodas and it's carried on since then. I tried to stop this addiction before, and don't recall having had any kind of withdrawal symptoms, but I always came back to it. Even as I write this, I can easily conjure up the taste and sensation of drinking a Diet Pepsi. This is something I've been doing, nearly unabated, for over 60 years.

My wife has pestered me about this habit for a long time, saying it was bad for me. But there was never anything concrete or compelling as to what "bad" meant, so I would brush those comments away and continue on, though temporarily cutting back on my 4-6 cans a day routine. I figured I was doing enough other positive things for my health that this one indiscretion was okay.

But when I read about the importance of telomeres, and about the things that can affect their lengths, I couldn't justify my habit any longer. I really do want and expect to live a very long time, so if something as specific as drinking sodas is known to be on the bad side of the scale, I had to suck it up and retire that habit.

To help me resist the pull of this, I now refer to sodas as "Poison." Since I started doing that, if I really, really want to have a soda, like if I've had crappy sleep and my eyelids are dragging on the floor (a common scenario at times in the past), I just have to announce that I will be buying and consuming poison. That usually shuts down the impulse, and the longer this poison is in my rearview mirror, the easier it is to live without it.

So what's your poison? What seems so integral to your existence that you can't imagine life without it — but that also happens to be bad for your long-term health? Is there only one thing, or do you have several poisons? How long are you willing to put your health at risk by continuing these habits?

I know from quitting my soda habit that it's not a straight line from "Oh, this really is bad for me and I need to do something about it" to "I'm done with that behavior forever." My dance with this has been two steps forward, one step back — until I labeled sodas as poison, and that made a huge difference.

In changing a significant habit, you'll want to be clear about why this is important to you, and you'll want to have support from family and friends. Check out *Tiny Habits* by BJ Fogg or *Atomic Habits* by James Clear for more detailed approaches to habit change.

Sleep

This needs no introduction — sleep is critical to life. What isn't widely known is that older people need as much sleep as anybody else; it's is a myth that we require less. People, as they age, may indeed sleep fewer hours than they used to, but it's not because their body is waking them up, saying "Hey, sleepyhead, here's a couple extra hours you could use!" There's always some root cause.

This is not super simple to solve, however; I know from personal experience. Over the past two years, I have often had problems getting adequate sleep. In my case, it's not the falling asleep part that's at issue, it's the waking up multiple times, struggling to fall back asleep, waking up too early, and feeling like I'd been run over by a truck when I do finally get up.

I have no idea what's going on or why. Too much alcohol? No. Food issues? No. Too much stimulation from TV or time on my phone? Rarely. Stresses in my life? Nope, and that seems like it would be more an issue in falling asleep, not staying asleep.

Breathing issues? Possibly. To check for sleep apnea, I endured a sleep study (one of the three worst nights of my life), briefly tried a CPAP machine (a life-saver for some people, but a disaster for me), and went to see a gaggle of doctors. I finally landed on an issue with the structure of my nose, which is eased by using BreatheRight nasal strips.

There are a number of other things I could check out or do (drop the temperature in the room, take a shower or bath before, take CBD pills, get a prescription for something stronger, and so on), but it's never gotten so bad that I haven't been able to function the next day. And, when I can, I'll take a 20-minute nap.

The key point is that insomnia is not normal as you get older. If you're having issues, get it checked out. Being sleep-deprived is a lousy state to be in, and as we get older it can also lead to cognitive decline, heart disease, and cancer.

Brain Health

Mental decline is one of the biggest fears people have about aging. Alzheimer's disease is the most dreaded, but memory loss, confusion, compromised reasoning, and depression are not far behind. The basic thinking is that if I lose my mind, who am I, and why would I want to go on living? What complicates this is the belief by many people that some or all of these impairments are inevitable, that we are hard-wired to have our brains decay.

It's not true that we are destined to suffer these losses, however, even with the knowledge that tens of millions of people are carrying preclinical evidence of Alzheimer's right now. That's right, lots of us have the potential to eventually develop Alzheimer's disease, but it's not certain who will get it and who won't. These preclinical conditions are something a brain scan can reveal, but individuals at this stage don't feel any effects. Dr. Sanjay Gupta, in his book *Keep Sharp: Build a Better Brain at Any Age,* has a great analogy for this: "It's like an approaching storm that is still way off in the distance, taking decades before memory, thinking, and behavior are affected." I would add that just because the storm is on the horizon does not mean the storm will stay on track to wallop you.

So, how do you outrun the storm of Alzheimer's disease and other mental impairments?

For starters, run — or at least walk. Sanjay Gupta says that just two minutes of activity every hour is one of the best things you can do for your brain, far better than swallowing a handful of brain-boosting supplements.

You can take this dedication to movement to a higher level by taking that walk with a friend, since social interactions pay huge dividends when it comes to brain health.

Reducing alcohol use, shifting to a plant-based diet, and getting sufficient sleep are also part of the prescription.

It may surprise you that things like doing crossword puzzles or sudoku, working in the garden, attending cultural events, or using the computer are *not* on the "Do This" list. The problem is that, while enjoyable, they don't tend to push your brain or challenge it in new ways, and that's something that is critical to protecting yourself from cognitive decline.

You need to find things that pull you out of your comfort zone, like learning a new language, developing new skills (ukulele anyone?), or interacting with people outside your usual circle of friends. Anything that forces your brain to work, to connect ideas, and to come up with novel solutions will help your brain grow, and it's that growth that is so important — at any and all ages. Yes, you can learn new tricks, even if you feel like an old dog. In fact, according to Gupta, significant upgrades can be made to the brain within just 12 weeks. Even aspects of memory can be improved as we age. For example, the ability to synthesize information, make decisions based on disparate data, and make accurate predictions improves over time because we've had so much life experience.

The key is to start now, not once you begin to notice cognitive impairments. And look beyond just your bucket list (if that's where your focus is) or your dates with your grandkids. Trips and projects and time with family are wonderful, but they're not likely to push your brain to create new neural connections. Gerontologist Ross Andel says that, "You might be particularly susceptible to cognitive decline when there's a lack of an activity to replace your occupation." He suggests finding a new activity that's meaningful to you and to others; we'll discuss this further in "Purpose" below.

Additional Considerations

Mindfulness: Slowing down, connecting with the present moment, tuning into yourself and the world around you, acknowledging and accepting your feelings — these states of being provide powerful ways to manage stress, increase awareness, build resilience, and support whole body health. More than just mere time-outs, they give you a chance to see things from new perspectives and tap sources of wisdom you might otherwise race past. Meditation is the most widely known way to begin a mindfulness practice, but you can achieve many of the same gains from walking in nature or having deep conversations with close friends.

Staying Up-to-Date: In our busy lives, it can be easy to postpone things like doctor visits, vaccinations, taking your blood pressure, or even just remembering to take your daily medications (if you take meds daily). But more than ever, as you age, it's critical to stay current on your checkups and have help identifying any variances or disruptions in an otherwise healthy life. Here's an example. Two years ago, my eye doctor said I was developing macular degeneration. WTF?! Impaired vision is one of the things I truly fear. I quietly freaked out inside, but managed to hear her recommend I take Lutein pills; I have been a diligent consumer of those pills every day since. I went recently for my latest check-up and was nervous about whether the macular degeneration had advanced. It hasn't! It has receded. Hallelujah! Take your meds, friend.

Dental Care: This might seem like an outlier here, but how well you take care of your teeth, particularly with regard to *flossing*, can have a massive impact on your health. Chronic inflammation is the concern, because it can lead to shortened telomeres, Alzheimer's, diabetes, hypertension, and heart disease. Inflamed gums, which flossing keeps at bay, can be a serious contributor to chronic inflammation elsewhere in your body. It's kind of mind blowing to think that not flossing could lead to heart problems or a cognitive decline, but that's how interconnected are our bodies. So see your dentist regularly and floss!

Fitness

Research — lots and lots of research — has clearly established that exercise and being fit are crucial to your health and longevity. Exercise helps your heart, your brain, the functioning of your organs, and so much more. It is the most prescribed treatment for illness and injury prevention and recovery. It is also critical to maintaining the health of your DNA defenders, the telomeres. Exercise gives you so much and, in its simplest form, walking, it asks so little. You just need to do it.

So where do you fall in the continuum of exercise and fitness? Are you a gym rat, a marathoner, or some other super committed exerciser? Or are you a couch potato, thinking it might be good to do at least some walking, but postponing it to an endless string of "tomorrows"?

My guess is that you're somewhere in between, but even if you're more toward the couch potato end of the scale, it's not too late. Even if you're 92, it's not too late. You just need to start. What follows are recommendations for wherever you are in your fitness journey right now, from base level to intermediate to advanced.

Base Level

Some of the advice you read or hear can feel daunting. The CDC's recommendation for physical activity is 150 minutes of moderate exercise per week (or 75 minutes of vigorous exercise), *plus* doing muscle-strengthening exercises twice a week. For a lot of people that kind of commitment, either in time or effort, can be a non-starter. I'm not saying you shouldn't strive to hit those objectives, but if it feels like this is an all-or-nothing proposition, well, you can probably understand why only 24% of Americans between 18 and 64 hit those numbers; the percentage is less for those over 65.

If you're already doing some kind of exercise regularly, great! You can skip down to the Intermediate or even the Advanced level.

For everyone else — those who've started and stopped, those who've been inconsistent, or those who've never really established an exercise routine, this doesn't have to be a hero-or-zero project. Just start. Start small.

As mentioned above, Dr. Sanjay Gupta says that just *two minutes* of movement each hour can do wonders for your brain, your heart, and everything else. This isn't something you need workout clothes or exercise equipment for, just get up and move. Go up and down the stairs four times. Do two laps around your floor at the office or, better yet, go outside and walk around the block. If you can do this movement briskly, not so that you break a sweat but so you elevate your heart rate a little, so much the better.

Taking a short break like that, in the midst of whatever you're doing, also pays huge dividends in your creativity and the clarity of your thinking. By getting outside of your normal work zone, you'll open up all kinds of new perspectives. I created most of two novels, not while sitting at my computer, but while doing deep water running at my health club.

To move this effort up a notch, consider that the Norwegian School of Sports Medicine, in a large, multi-year study, determined that just 11 minutes of moderate exercise a day can give you long-term health benefits and increased longevity. The greatest benefits, particularly in joint health, were found in those who did 35 minutes a day, but even just 11 minutes a day provided benefits. Their examples of moderate exercise included walking, major cleaning (something vigorous like vacuuming or mopping), mowing the lawn, or doing a light bike ride.

So get started. Any movement is better than no movement. At this level, there should be no excuses for not doing this — and big reasons for doing some kind of exercise every day.

Intermediate

Yay you for making exercise and fitness a priority! You're improving your health every time you get in motion. Now let's take things further. If you're not doing so already, there are three areas to focus on: aerobics or cardio; strength training; and balance and flexibility.

Aerobic Exercise: This gets your heart rate elevated, either from increased intensity of effort or from sustained effort above your normal level of exertion. Since you're already at this level, you probably don't need a run-down on what to do. The big thing is to workout at a brisk pace. This isn't about going all-out; that would be anaerobic exercise, which you'll find in the Advanced level. For now, just get your heart pumping for an extended period of time; a leisurely walk with a friend, while nice, doesn't qualify here.

How long to exercise depends on your situation. You really should try to meet or exceed the guidelines that CDC has set — 150 minutes per week of moderate exercise or 75 minutes of vigorous exercise — but you can divide that up any way you like. Do you have an hour to go for a hike? Great! Do you have only 15 minutes free? Go for a run or a fast walk. Quality definitely beats quantity. As for the suggestion that you should get 10,000 steps every day, it's your choice. If having that goal pushes you to reach it each day, do it. But if you burn 300 or more calories swimming, you don't also need to hit that 10k level of steps.

Do what you feel drawn to, get your heart pumping, and mix it up so you don't get bored. And if you can't do something every day, don't sweat it. Just restart the next day.

Strength Training: This is so important, but it's also widely ignored. CDC statistics from 2015 showed that 43% of people age 65-74 met the guidelines for *aerobic* activity, while only 22% of that group met the strength training goal of two times per week. And all those percentages drop as people get older.

There are probably lots of reasons for the low numbers: it hurts; it's inconvenient; gyms are only for younger people; I'll go once I lose 10 pounds (my dad's standard line); it's expensive; I'll look stupid or wimpy with my low weights.

And all those reasons are BS. Gyms are not just for younger people, it doesn't have to be expensive (see below), going to the gym might be the thing to help you lose those 10 pounds, and who cares what you look like anyway? This isn't a beauty contest or a fashion show, and there's no winner at the end of the day — except you because you stepped up to do the work.

There is a gift in the pain you might feel (if you don't overdo things), because that means your body is growing. It means your bones are becoming more dense, your muscles are getting stronger, your alignment is getting better, your resilience is increasing, your blood pressure and cholesterol are probably dropping, and so much more. Strength training provides gains that aerobic exercise can't match, and it's a critical part of living an active, vital life until your last days.

So how do you get started? The ideal scenario would be to find a gym nearby, the closer the better so you have one less reason not to go. You'll find a wide variety of equipment and likely a friendly trainer who can help you design a program. (More on this below.)

If it seems too expensive to join a gym, and if you're 65 or older, there's a fantastic program called SilverSneakers that gives you free entrance to over 14,000 facilities across the United States. I was put off by it at first because of, well, "Silver." I thought SilverSneakers would be a bunch of really old people shuffling around a rec room, but boy was I wrong. This is a program run by Medicare and supported by insurance companies, and it really does provide free access to gyms and rec centers all over the U.S. It doesn't pay for trainers or certain classes, but I've gone from spending hundreds of dollars a year for entry to zero dollars a year — at my regular gym — and there are a dozen participating facilities within a 10-minute drive from my house.

If a gym environment just isn't your thing, no worries. You can buy some modest weights to use at home — or you can make your own. Do curls with jugs of milk, or flys with cans of beans. You can find lots of ideas and routines online.

The one thing you should spend a little money on is a few sessions with a certified trainer, particularly one who has worked with older people. You'll benefit from having a professional design a program that will challenge you, but not break you. I had an unfortunate experience a few years back with a guy who had me doing a lot of work with a barbell at weights that proved too much for me. So ask a lot of questions and make sure you feel compatible with this person. You're putting your body in their hands.

How often should you go? Twice a week is a great way to start; I currently go three times a week, mixing that with swimming and hiking on the other days. If you find that you're really enjoying the sensation of pushing yourself, and if you're enjoying the fresh and stronger way you feel, you don't have to hold back. There are lots of stories about people, even into their 90s, who are doing amazing things with strength training. Charles Eugster didn't start lifting weights until he was 85, but he really took to it and ultimately entered and won several age-group competitions. There's a picture of him at 91, wearing a collection of medals and with *massive* arms. My arms have never looked like that, even when I was in the weight room a lot during my triathlon days; the fact that I wasn't trying to get arms like that is beside the point — I can't even imagine my arms looking that way. It is NOT too late to get started.

Balance and Flexibility: Working on your balance and flexibility keeps your body running smoothly in the midst of all you're doing, whether exercising or just getting through a busy day. Improving your balance and flexibility reduces the risk of falls and other injuries, decreases chronic pain, improves coordination and posture, helps you perform better, and lets you recover faster from hard workouts. When I was doing triathlons and marathons, and training madly when I wasn't racing, my saviors were 30 minutes of stretching each day and getting a massage once a week.

There is no magical formula for working on your balance and flexibility, you just need to devote the time to it. There are tools that can help you, like balance boards, Swiss balls, and foam rollers, but you can do everything you need just with your body. There are thousands of books and YouTube videos that will help you choose a routine that works for you.

There are also many types of classes that can help you develop your balance and flexibility, including yoga, tai chi, and Pilates. You may also find classes at your local gym that focus specifically on balance and flexibility. Classes offer the advantage of a structure to guide you, so you don't have to create it yourself. You'll also have people going through the class with you, and that shared effort provides a huge boost as you're working through a challenging class.

The key thing is to work on your balance and flexibility, no matter how you do that. And be consistent. Doing this work sporadically will not provide the gains that regular, consistent focus provides. Your body wants to be loose and supple — give it what it needs.

Advanced

At this level, you don't need much guidance from me. Your program is already well established. But here are some ideas that may help you get more out of your time, or that can add variety to what you're doing.

Anaerobic Work: If you're not pushing yourself occasionally into your red zone, you might be limiting your growth. This is particularly important if you're competing, which a lot of older people are doing now — in road races, triathlons, track and field, swimming, cycling, rowing, and more. Anaerobic work shakes up your system and blows out the cobwebs of a static routine. When you force your body towards its limits, it responds by creating new connections and new cells to help you achieve your goal. You don't want to do this work every session, but periodic use of, say, high-intensity interval training (aka HIIT) pays huge dividends. Check this out if you're not doing some kind of anaerobic work already.

Workout Partner: Having someone to train with is one of the best things you can do to keep your motivation strong and your enjoyment high. Even if there's an element of suffering in what you're doing, that shared sense of meeting adversity makes a hard effort significantly more tolerable and achievable. A training partner will keep you accountable for showing up and not wimping out, and will support you when you need it.

Goals: Having something that you're training for is incredibly motivating. It makes you excited to do another workout, even if a particular session seems like a monster. When I was training for a half-Ironman triathlon (or a 70.3, as it's now called), part of my training plan a few weeks before the event was to do a 70-mile bike ride, followed immediately by a 10-mile run. I knew this workout would be several hours of pain, but the lure of competing in that race was so strong that this was just part of what I needed to do. And I got through it and had a blast in the race. So find something you love to do that will be a stretch — maybe a race in some exotic location or your first marathon — and let that be the prize that drives you onward.

Cross Training: Adding variety to your exercise regime makes you better able to excel in your sport of choice. You'll increase your flexibility, your resilience, and your passion for the work you're doing. So if you're a cyclist, try swimming or rowing. If you're a trail runner, get on a bike. The options are limitless. And your growth is, too, the more you shake your body out of its routine.

Prioritize Recovery: It's one thing to perform hard; it's another to perform well and do it consistently. Your body needs downtime in order to rebuild from the efforts it's put in. Sleep is the best recovery choice, but massage, stretching, foam rollers, and hot tubs all help break up the stiffness you're likely feeling.

Don't Go Crazy: There's a tendency, when you're working out hard, to think you need to — or *get to* — pile on the calories after a session. You know that feeling, that "I've earned this" or "I deserve this" urge to do a face plant into, say, a pile of donuts. And refueling *is* important, particularly in the first 30 minutes, but resist the urge to absolutely let go. Be strategic about what you put back into your body, with protein, electrolytes, and high quality carbs (think banana, not bagel). You don't want to undo all the good you've just done for your body.

Mindset

Emmy Award-winning actress Patricia Heaton, in a 2020 interview with AARP Magazine, said, "Being 62 is great! With mortality even more present now and the end looming, you realize, I don't need to do anything I don't want to do. I don't have to tolerate people who aren't good for me."

That last part, the sense of advocating for herself, is great, but what's up with "THE END IS LOOMING"?! The emphasis is mine, of course, and I would hope it's yours, too. The end is looming at age 62? The definition of "looming" includes a time-based qualifier as something horrible that is *about to happen.* Really, Patricia?

This is a mindset that is not going to get you far. How free and expansive can you be about your future if you feel that death is imminent? To the contrary, it would either make you curl up like a pill bug to protect yourself or have you throw caution completely to the wind while awaiting some dark force to pounce on you. Living in the moment is important, but it's not useful as your only strategy for getting through 30 years or so.

Maybe her comment was influenced by pandemic-related fears. A couple times during 2020, I had some vague fears, but I never once thought a horrible death was just about to claim me and thus I'd better get busy on my bucket list, in a socially-distant way.

Or perhaps Patricia was just being flip, but there's usually an element of truth to comments like that. I'm less concerned about her, though, than I am about you. The more I can help you face the future in a way that's bursting with life, rather than expecting an impending death, the more you'll do, the better you'll feel, the more you'll contribute to the world, and the better an example you'll set for generations to come. That doesn't mean you should put on rose colored glasses and dance around like nothing bad could ever happen to you — we will talk at the end of this chapter about realistic perspectives — but when your guiding principle is that death is lurking nearby, it can have an adverse effect on your mind, your body, and your spirit.

In counterpoint to Patricia's riff, let's look at research that Ellen Langer did at Harvard in the 1981. Curious about how social context affects aging, she designed what is known as the Counterclockwise Study. With two groups of men in their late 70s, those in the experimental group were asked to act *as if* they were living in 1959, not 1981. For a week they lived in an environment that was straight out of the 1950s — in the clothes they wore, the music they listened to, the food they ate, the TV shows they watched — and they were asked to not discuss modern day events or circumstances. The control group, by contrast, was asked to merely reminisce about the past.

At the end of the study, the experimental group showed significant improvement in memory, dexterity, eyesight, hearing, and other factors that often deteriorate with age. Those who used canes when they arrived walked away without them, and they carried their own suitcases rather than rely on family who had assisted them earlier. The reminiscing control group did not realize similar improvements.

Shawn Achor's TEDTalk on "The Happy Secret to Better Work," with more than 23 million views, included this fascinating statistic: "90% of your long-term happiness is predicted not by the external world, but by the way your brain processes the world."

Basically, your thoughts create your world. And there's no expiration date on choosing to view life however you want.

Researchers at Harvard discovered that optimists live 11% to 15% longer than less optimistic people. Researchers at Johns Hopkins Medicine found that people with a family history of heart disease who had a positive outlook were one-third less likely to have a heart attack within five to 25 years than those with a negative outlook.

And what does that have to do with optimizing your life? Don't buy into the idea that frailty, mental decline, and a life of decay and irrelevancy are awaiting you — or that the end is looming.

If you don't want to be old, don't think of yourself as old. Don't attribute anything that happens to you as being a result of aging. And refuse to accept it when someone, usually in a patronizing tone, utters lines like "You're too old to _____." "At your age?" "What do you expect, you're old." and so on. Screw that crap.

Yes, your body will change over time, but you don't have to tell yourself stories that make you the victim of aging's mighty sword. Why choose to feel bad? Your brain is a freaking, supercharged marvel, capable of things way beyond your expectations — particularly at your age!

If you want examples of people who are not letting aging run their lives, check out a charming book by Ari Seth Cohen called *Advanced Style*. It shows, in glossy photos, a parade of New Yorkers who, while older, are dressed *fabulously*. Nobody looks dour or drab or OLD — wrinkled, yes, but boy do their spirits light up the pages. The clothes are probably freaking expensive, but it's the energy each of them exudes that makes the images radiant. You could dress them in potato sacks and they'd carry it off with style; the zest in these pictures is timeless. As one woman said, "When you are younger, you dress for other people. When you are older, you dress for yourself."

And that's the point. Let your inside shine and your outside will be amazing to your last breath, regardless of your clothing budget. Do what you want, no matter what anyone else thinks. *That* is how you conquer aging, by making it irrelevant.

Purpose

Which of these best defines your outlook?

1) "I live life one day at a time and don't really think about the future."

2) "I sometimes feel like I've done all there is to do in life."

3) "Some people wander aimlessly through life, but I am not one of them."

On the Ryff Scale of Psychological Well-Being, created by Carol Ryff at the University of Wisconsin, one sentence helps promote a longer, healthier life, and the other two can lead to increased risks of major diseases and a shortened life span.

Before I give you the answer, I want to note that these three ideas align with some of the stages of retirement that we looked at earlier.

The first sentence expresses the excitement upon retiring of having no job, no schedule, no responsibilities, and no pressure. It seems attractive to have nothing to do when your life has been structured for decades. Sure, maybe you'll work a little bit in your retirement, and definitely spend time with the grandchildren, but being free is kind of the point. Wake up whenever, do whatever, go wherever, be however. It's the release so many people crave.

The second sentence describes the state many people reach, somewhere between six months and three years after retiring. "Retirement Hell" is how Mike Drak and Jonathan Chevreau termed this phase, in their book of the same name. The thing about this state, where you go from blissfully aimless to what-am-I-doing-with-my-life, is that you don't reach it overnight. It's a gradual change, which can be accompanied by depression, cognitive impairment, and greater risks of heart disease, stroke, diabetes, and obesity — things that lower your quality of life and reduce your health and life span. And once those things get a toehold in your body and your brain, it's much harder to get rid of them.

The third sentence speaks to a time after escaping from retirement hell, when people have found a new direction for their life. In large measure, what's different here is having a sense of purpose — a reason to get up in the morning on a regular basis, in service of something bigger than just a day's casual adventure.

In case you were still wondering, the longevity-promoting sentence is the third one. Research has shown that those with higher levels of purpose in their life are at reduced risk for Alzheimer's disease, heart attack, stress, and inflammation, as well as all the maladies mentioned just above. Researchers even found that having a higher sense of purpose buffered those who suffering from serious illnesses and chronic diseases.

Does this mean that "purpose" equals "full-time job?" No, not at all. Purpose can come in the form of doing volunteer work, mentoring people, writing books, developing courses on topics that inspire you, creating photo essays to support causes that are important to you, spending more time with a spiritual community, joining a startup company, or almost anything.

What purpose does equal is a longer life and a better life.

We'll get deeper into how to develop and nurture your purpose in the *Defining Your New Path* chapter, but it's important to recognize here the importance for your health span and your life span of having *something* to which you're devoted.

Social Connections

There's an insidious thing that happens to many people as they get older. Their health and mobility decline, friends move away or pass away, their neighborhood changes, and it becomes harder and harder to maintain regular contact with other human beings. This can become particularly acute if you are living alone.

The net effect? Isolation increases, social interactions become more limited, and a host of health problems creep in: depression; cognitive decline; physical decline; cardiovascular issues; obesity and diabetes; osteoporosis; and more. Risk factors for loneliness increase as well, which only worsens the spiral. According to several studies, these effects raise your mortality risk by up to 32%, on a par with the risks from obesity, smoking, and alcoholism for illness and early death.

Having regular contact with others — family, friends near or far, and even just passing interactions with, say, the barista at a coffee shop — reverses the likelihood of such bad occurrences. Something about human interaction, as brief as it may be, buoys us. People who feel more connected are healthier, more mobile, more engaged, and more resilient.

In fact, a study by Lisa Berkman and S. Leonard Syme found that people who had close social ties, but an unhealthy lifestyle (e.g. alcoholism, smoking, or lack of exercise), lived longer than those who had a healthy lifestyle, but poor social ties.

So maintaining contact with others is critical as you age. Sometimes that's easy, if you live with someone or have close friends nearby, but even then it's important to stay vigilant, even dedicated, to keeping the social fires burning. And pay attention to connections beyond your most immediate circle. Variety of interactions is good for you.

That doesn't mean you need to be packing your calendar to the limit; sometimes just a quick "Hello" in the grocery store can shift the course of your day, and the person you're connecting with.

One of the keys, though, is being deliberate about maintaining and strengthening your relationships, and creating new ones. If you wait for others to knock on your door, literally or figuratively, you might be waiting a long time, and your health will suffer.

This part is easy for extroverts like my wife; she can talk to anyone about anything at any time. For those on the introvert side of the scale, like me, it takes a bit more effort sometimes to engage people in conversation, but it's always worth it. Once, while my wife and I were waiting at the airport, I mentioned to a guy nearby that he had a spectacular beard — and it truly was. That one comment sparked a fascinating, hour-long conversation with him and his business partner about beards and robotics and so much more. That experience reminds me that I need to engage people more often.

A major factor in how socially engaged you are is where you live. Let's look at the primary choices ahead of you.

Aging in Place: Researchers have found that a majority of people, as they get older, want to "age in place" — that is, to continue to live in the same place they've been, even if that house, condo, or apartment might present difficulties in their later years. I confess that I look at the stairs in our house sometimes and wonder if going up and down them multiple times a day might be a problem at some point.

There are great advantages to aging in place, though. We develop attachments to places and people and the routines of daily life, and not disrupting those while dealing with other life changes means that we still have some stability and choice in our lives. If you really love where you live and appreciate all that you have around you, that supports your health and longevity.

But if you're hanging on to some place out of habit or a fear of change, even if your life is more difficult or insular by staying where you've been, then that is degrading your health, your longevity, and potentially your safety.

Habit, tradition, and control are big deals at any time, but particularly as we age. When it feels like so much is being taken away from you, it's natural to want to hold on to *something* that is meaningful or represents your deepest feelings about your life. For my mom, that was dining room chairs.

In her last 17 years, she moved three times. First from the four-bedroom house I grew up in to a charming two-bedroom house in a little enclave near a friend, to a smaller two-bedroom apartment that was utilitarian at best, to her final place, a sunny, but tiny one-bedroom apartment in a pleasant assisted-living facility. With each move, she had to let go of some of her furniture, purely for space reasons.

The final move was the hardest, because the place was so small. Mom and I got into a heated exchange about the number of chairs for her antique dining room set she could bring into the new apartment. I knew only four would fit; she angrily insisted on the full set of eight. We finally reached a compromise — four chairs would go to a storage shed my sister had, to be retrieved if needed — but Mom's desperation never left me. It wasn't just the chairs, of course, though her sense of propriety was strong. It was also a sign that she would probably not be hosting big, spontaneous gatherings any longer, and that was particularly painful for her.

There are other things to be aware of, if you choose to age in place. These aren't fun topics or easy decisions, but you'll be way ahead if you sort them out before you have to. Here's a starter set:

- Does your house need updates to make it more aging-friendly, with things like grab bars in the shower, a bedroom on the main floor, adequate clearance should you need to move around in a wheel chair at some point?

- Who can you call on, at short notice, if you need assistance in the home or to get to medical appointments?

- What kind of transportation options do you have, for when you can't drive any longer, or if you can't navigate the steps or stairs for various types of public transportation?

- How about meals, household chores, and personal care? Who will remind you about taking your medications?

- How will you stay connected to others if you end up home-bound?

We could generate a long list pretty quickly. Some of these considerations will be in force no matter where you live, though they're likely to be more pressing if you are aging in place, particularly if you're living alone.

Hopefully none of these things will be an issue for you for a long time, but it's better to work out some of these details in advance of needing an urgent solution. And if you can get everything sorted out, including your social contacts, in a way that supports you adequately while aging in place, that could be a wonderful approach.

Aging in Community: The alternative to aging in place is being part of a community, whether loosely, such as in retirement havens like Sun

City and the Villages in Florida, or in a controlled environment like assisted living. My mom flourished in assisted living, though she probably wasn't ready for it when she was more able to care for herself.

There are a couple other options, however — multigenerational arrangements and a village concept — that sound really intriguing.

A multigenerational approach has so much to recommend it. Being able to mix generations pays huge dividends to everyone — the grandparents, who get to be much more involved with their children and grandchildren and engage in a diversity of ideas and conversations, the middle generation, who have ready support in managing the family and who get more quality time with their parents, and the younger ones, who get more time with grandparents *and* observe a better model for healthy aging than society continues to feed us. Sure, there can be some issues around boundaries, but this is more a question of design than it is any basic failings of this approach. The best scenario I've heard is, rather than having everyone under one roof, having two or three houses close together so that it's easy to mix things up, between private time and big, communal gatherings.

The village concept involves a collection of smaller houses grouped in close proximity, often with a central square or meeting house. You can be as private as you want, but other people are as close as your front door. Activities can be shared and it's easier to support one another's needs. Expenses are shared for services that benefit everyone, and if you need help with moving a couch or getting to the doctor, there's probably someone nearby.

Another benefit is that, if you're around people who exercise, get regular checkups, and are focused on healthy aging, you're more likely to do the same. They become not just a model, but also a partner in living a more enriching life. Having a community like this helps sustain you when close family live far away. I wouldn't be surprised if my wife and I ended up in this type of situation.

Making New Connections: Throughout this section on Social Contact, the key idea is interacting with other people. Relationships provide so many benefits for your current and long-term health. If you're aging in place, you've probably got a solid group of friends and perhaps family nearby.

But if you move or your social circle reduces, it's important to find and develop new friendships. One of the best ways to do this is to volunteer your time and expertise to some cause you care about. That "care about" part is critical, since you'll feel so much more invested when you're contributing to something that's meaningful to you.

Think about where you might be of service *or* where you might need help. I once volunteered to assist people in preparing their income taxes, because I knew that in the training, I would be able to get my own questions answered. I had a blast doing it.

And don't be afraid to just talk to someone. My experience with the guy with the spectacular beard happened because I went from *thinking* about speaking up to actually speaking up. He didn't look the kind of person I might normally chat with — he had this grungy biker look — but I was so intrigued by his beard I had to speak up. And he was pleased by my observation. We had a great conversation, and it was a significantly better use of my time than thumbing mindlessly through my phone.

As you get older, don't shrink from life. Don't sit and wait for someone to knock on your door. Go out and find people, find things to do, find ways to be useful to others. It is in that sharing that you build connection and vitality in your life.

Finances

This will be short, since there are thousands of people better qualified than me to advise you on how to set up your finances for the latter part of your life. I do have some personal experience, however, that's worth exploring regarding not running out of money, which is the #1 fear for many people. It was my mom's situation, but I had a ringside seat.

Through the 25 years of her second marriage, Mom never paid attention to her finances; that was her husband's job. After he died, she left all that stewardship to a wealth manager who, during the 2008 market crash, was *not* paying attention to her account and she lost 50%

of the value of her estate. She had stopped working years before and, at 80 and in declining health, didn't have a long enough timeline to rebuild her holdings.

Thus began a series of moves, as mentioned above. When we started planning the last move, it was difficult to figure out where she could live. There wasn't any way to preserve her principal, if we moved her to one of the assisted living places she'd hoped to get into (and which she needed). So it was a sad, strange experience for me to create an actuarial table on my mom, trying to figure out how long she might live, what her budget should be, and thus what she could spend for rent and services.

Things worked out okay, though it was hard to tell my mom that the only gifts she could afford to give now were her time and her love, not anything that cost money. And she wouldn't have all the amenities she'd once had. But she lived six more years in a pleasant environment, with me anxiously watching her bank balance every month.

Don't let yourself get to that point. If you need to keep working to support yourself for 30 years, go ahead. It's not a failing if you do. Stay aware of your financial situation and get advice from a competent financial professional about timing of withdrawals, which accounts to tap when, and so on. Keep a cushion of cash available. Downsize if you need to. Hopefully all that will keep you as worry-free as possible. Removing those kinds of stress will boost your health immeasurably.

Being Realistic

Finally, you need to acknowledge that some things may break down in your body, despite all your best efforts to keep bad things at bay. Trying to will these issues away through the powers of your mind may not be sufficient. So the questions then are what do you need to do, and how do you want to be with these setbacks? The more you can find clarity and a sense of control, the better able you'll be to navigate difficult situations.

We'll leave questions of how to handle harsh diagnoses to other books and resources. The whole point of this chapter is not to make you invincible — hell, we're all going to die at some point. Instead, it's about optimizing your health, both physical and mental, so that you can make the most of every day you have on this planet and keep illness and decline at bay as long as possible.

There's a term for this: Compressed Morbidity. It's the idea that you want your health span, the period in which you're in relatively good health, to be as long as your life span, which is the number of days you live. The more compressed is your morbidity, the fewer days you'll spend seriously ill before you die.

There's a woman you'll meet in the next chapter, Olga Kotelko, who was setting world records in track and field events into her 90s. A week before her death at 95, she competed in three track events at a regional meet. Shortly after returning home, while she was asleep, a blood vessel in her brain burst and she died three days later. That's a powerful example of compressed morbidity.

May your health span be similarly long, long, long.

You have the power to make it so.

What will you commit to doing to improve your longevity?

1)

2)

3)

How to Be a Badass in Your 80s & 90s

The question isn't "Who's going to let me?"
It's "Who's going to stop me?"
· Ayn Rand ·

If you ask people about the word "badass," they're likely to mention an actor or a character in a movie — Bruce Lee, Shaft, Sarah Conner in *The Terminator*, John McClain in *Die Hard* — someone who seems larger-than-life and has an outsized impact on the world. A badass may not wear a cape like a superhero or have magical powers, but through grit, ingenuity, and commitment to their cause, they prevail. It's not a question of *if* they'll survive, but *how.*

Real badasses are all around us, though few are brawny or toting a gun. Look at former President Jimmy Carter, who at 95 helped build a house for Habitat for Humanity *the day after* getting 14 stitches to close up a gash over his eye. Or 80 year-old Anthony Fauci, who put in 19-hour days for almost a year to help the U.S. navigate the Covid-19 pandemic. And consider all the unsung frontline workers who daily faced possible infection and even death to try to save people ravaged by Covid-19. Heros all, even if they wore PPE, or sometimes trash bags, instead of capes.

We need to celebrate the badasses of the world, not just because they do hard, dangerous, or mind-blowing things. It's their conviction, vulnerability, and heart that elevate them from merely "accomplished" or "significant" to "badass." And it's in how they chart their own course. They show us that we, too, can be a force for good in the world. They give us glimpses of a better version of ourselves.

You absolutely have it in you to be a badass, to be an important influence on others, whether that collection of others is a small circle of friends or millions of people around the world. It's not the size of your reach that matters, it's the depth of your impact. We're talking agent-of-change here, not merely social media influencer.

So why would you want to be a badass? It shouldn't be about the title — that's for others to proclaim, not you; if you declare that you're a badass, you're probably not. Instead, this is about being so deeply invested in something you're passionate about that you would move heaven and earth to keep pursuing it. There's no question of quitting, no feeling swayed by the opinions of others, and no being stopped by the voices in your head telling you can't or shouldn't do something. It's an exhilarating way to go through life.

And that sense of mission is obvious to the people you encounter, or those who hear about you. It captures their attention, but it also registers on a deeper, more visceral level. And it leaves them feeling, "Wow, she's amazing!"

Most people won't be interested in being a badass; some might even shun the idea. I would hope, however, that everyone who draws a breath would want to be filled up with *something* they care about. And if you keep pursuing it, and increasing your commitment, overcoming obstacles that try to hold you back, forging ahead when others have faltered, and reaching levels of accomplishment no one could have imagined, well . . . you've probably shown the world something new, something unexpected, and something redeeming. And in the process, you've become a badass.

There is no age limit on when you can become a badass, nor does badassness expire after a certain date. Badass is badass, regardless of age, gender, color, or creed.

Here's a collection of badasses, all in their 80s or 90s, who show that you can do remarkable things and have a big impact at any age — and starting from any age.

Opal Lee · Activist

Opal Lee, or Ms. Opal as she likes to be called, loved the Juneteenth celebrations when she was a little girl in Texas. These were local affairs, similar to Independence Day gatherings in the community, but June 19th commemorates the day when slaves in Texas were finally freed, two-and-a-half years after Abraham Lincoln signed the Emancipation Proclamation.

These might have stayed local celebrations had it not been for Ms. Opal leading a crusade to get Juneteenth recognized as a national holiday, on par with July 4th and Labor Day.

She wasn't always such a firebrand. She didn't get involved in community causes until she ended her teaching career at age 50. Among her projects were helping to organize Fort Worth's annual celebration of Martin Luther King, Jr's birthday, Black History Month, and Juneteenth celebrations.

But she began to feel that Juneteenth needed to be more than a collection of local celebrations, that it could have greater significance for African Americans. She also felt it could open up awareness and opportunities to fight homelessness, secure decent housing and food for underprivileged people, and expand educational opportunities.

So she began, at age 89, a concerted push to get Juneteenth the recognition she felt it deserved. She launched a plan to walk from Fort Worth, Texas to Washington, D.C. in 2.5 mile increments, in recognition of the two-and-a-half years it took for slaves in Texas to learn they were free. She didn't actually walk the whole 1300 mile route, but did ceremonial walks in cities all over the country. And as she walked, she collected signatures — more than 1.5 million signatures in support of making Juneteenth a national holiday.

It took five years and multiple trips to Washington, but finally, at age 94, the "Grandmother of Juneteenth," as she's been called, sat in the front row as President Joe Biden signed into law the proclamation making Juneteenth a national holiday.

After the ceremony, she said the signing of the bill was just the beginning, and she added, "Nobody is free until we're all free."

Jeri Lampman · Cancer Survivor

Jeri Lampman is a badass on a smaller, but important scale. If you've ever seen the movie *Alien*, where the character Ripley battles a hideous alien that kills off her colleagues and tries to kill her as well, that's like Jeri and cancer. Her father died from lung cancer when she was in her 20s. Her son died of lymphoma when he was 31. Her husband died of cancer of the kidneys a few years later. Just months after her husband died, Jeri was diagnosed with breast cancer. In fact, she's survived cancer five times now!

In addition to caring for her son, her husband, and then herself while in treatment, Jeri also presided over the care and well-being of her mother, her daughter-in-law, and her two grandsons. When she couldn't find answers she'd been seeking about treatments during her husband's illness, she wrote a book, *Sharing Cancer: A Guide for Patients and Caregivers*, to help others on this journey. She travels around the country speaking about surviving cancer, runs cancer support groups, and participates in fund raising programs for cancer victims and their families. In her spare time, she has written novels, loves gardening, and went zip lining in her early 70s. Now, just shy of 80, when no one would begrudge her railing at the world, she is still focused on helping people in any way she can. She is an incredible role model for how to persevere under extreme conditions, and how to keep your spirits up. As she said at the end of our call, "Nobody has to act their age."

Eddy Goldfarb · Inventor

When he was six years old, Eddy Goldfarb knew what he wanted to be as an adult — an inventor. It was much later when that idea coalesced into what would be his life's work. While serving on a submarine during World War II, dreaming up inventions in every free moment, he decided that if he was going to be an independent inventor, not tied down to one company, he needed to specialize in one industry. Eddy chose toys.

He had his first big hit in 1949, with the introduction of Yakkity-Yak Teeth, a wind-up toy that chatters away as it skitters across a table. You've almost certainly seen one, and maybe even owned one at some point in your life. They are still being sold today, and derivative wind-up toys are everywhere. I remember having one of his toys when I was about eight years old, a Vac U Form press sold by Mattel.

Eddy has created more than 800 toys. You'd think with that track record, he might stop at some point, but as he approaches his 100th birthday, he still goes out every day to the machine shop he set up in his garage, dreaming up new toys for the latest generation of kids. There's something about spreading joy to families that still gets to him.

This singular commitment to his work is a key part of what's kept him going for eight decades as an inventor. In a documentary on his life, he says, "When you do creative work, you stimulate your brain, and that keeps your body healthy."

Olga Kotelko · Athlete

There's an amazing photo of Olga Kotelko, flying through the air above a long jump pit. She looks suspended, weightless, with excellent form and perfectly in command of the moment. She was 94 when the picture was taken.

Somewhere along the way, the clock seemed to have stopped on Olga's aging. Sure, her face looked like that of an older woman, but her energy and fire just burned brighter with each new year. She took up softball at age 70 to keep from being bored in retirement, and even turned a double play, but she left the sport at age 77 to focus on track and field events; these sports made better use of her running and throwing skills.

During the next 18 years, she amassed 30 world records and over 750 gold medals from meets all over the world. Granted, there wasn't a lot of competition in some of the age-groups she competed in (like 90-94), but physiological testing put her age-adjusted accomplishments on a par with elite athletes several decades younger. She was often just competing against her earlier records.

It's kind of crazy to see a 94-year old doing shot put and hammer throw, but Olga powers through them. (You'll find lots of these videos in YouTube.) She also competed in 100M, 200M, and 400M runs, as well as long jump, triple jump, discus, javelin, high jump, and the 4x100 relay.

She was still competing at 95 when, a week after a regional meet, she suffered a cerebral hemorrhage and died. She left behind a legacy and a badass approach to life that will be hard to equal. As she said once, "Growing old happens whether we like it or not, so why not make the best of these years?"

Shirley Curry · YouTube Gamer

You never know when inspiration will strike, nor exactly how it will manifest. And passion is even more mysterious. Shirley Curry wasn't thinking about any of this five years into her retirement, when her son introduced her to the computer game, Civilization II. She was just seized by the game and played it as much as she could.

There was nothing in her earlier years that would have signaled what was to come. While raising four children, she also worked as a secretary, on a candy-factory line, and in the clothing department at Kmart. She retired at 55 and, I guess, did retirement-y stuff.

Then her son introduced her to Civilization II, and ultimately she moved on to Skyrim, where she started to make her mark. At age 75, she joined YouTube and started uploading Skyrim-related videos. For most people starting a YouTube channel, it takes a long time before they get any real visibility. But Shirley's first video, where she does battle with a giant spider, got more than two million views!

In the next ten years, she would upload more than 1600 videos, garner more than 20 million views, and build a subscriber base of almost one million people. That is a rarified place on YouTube. And at 85, she's still going strong. She makes money off of her channel, but that's never been her primary driver. She just loves what she's doing and refers to all of her viewers as her grandkids.

Her fans are ardent supporters who don't care what she looks like or how old she is, calling her a "legend" and a "national treasure." Not bad for someone who was casually introduced to gaming, long after she'd retired. But she's found fame a bit overwhelming at times, particularly in trying to reply to the thousands of comments on her videos. Still, as she said in an interview with the New York Times, "Sometimes I get so tired, I feel like I'm going to quit this. But I can't, I just can't."

William Shatner · Actor

If you look at the older actors still doing incredible work — people like James Earl Jones (90), Maggie Smith (86), and Anthony Hopkins (83), who won his second Oscar for Best Actor in 2020 — you might wonder why William Shatner is featured here. Yes, he became a cultural icon from playing Captain Kirk on the original *Star Trek*, but he doesn't have quite the prominence that these and other actors have.

But that's what makes him so interesting in this discussion. Being a badass isn't about being the best at something, it's about being the best *you* — regardless of what others do or what others may say about you. It's about following a passion that burns white hot, and that speaks to so much of what William Shatner has done.

He can be a polarizing figure, but whether you love him, find him comical, or dislike him is irrelevant to him. He's just focused on whatever inspires him at the moment. If you like it, great. If you don't like it, that's cool. He seems to be enjoying life, no matter what the world thinks.

And, at 90, he's still testing his limits. He could have stayed in the safe haven of being an actor, but he's also been a best-selling author, recording artist, producer, director, scriptwriter, and CEO of a special effects studio. Each one of those provided a risk of failing. He did them anyway.

He also breeds and shows American Saddlebreds and Quarter Horses, and competes in "reining" competitions (like figure skating on a horse). He still rides motorcycles. And he continues to perform, recently diving with sharks for the Discovery Channel's latest Shark Week series — at 90! How badass is that?

As for the future, here's what he said about the final frontier in his book *Live Long And* . . . "Other people may accept death peacefully. Not me. When I go, I'm going kicking and screaming. I'm holding onto the furniture. And until that time, on a daily basis, I do as much as possible to stay fully engaged with the world."

He's the perfect embodiment of the famous Hunter S. Thompson quote: "Life should not be a journey to the grave with the intention of arriving safely in a pretty and well-preserved body, but rather to skid in broadside in a cloud of smoke, thoroughly used up, totally worn out, and loudly proclaiming, 'Wow! What a ride!'"

Wally Funk · Aviator/Astronaut

By almost every measure, Mary Wallace ("Wally") Funk, has had an incredible life. Fascinated by planes since she was a toddler, she got her pilot's license at age 17, became a flight instructor at 22, was the first female Flight Inspector and first female Air Safety Investigator for the Federal Aviation Administration (FAA) in her early 30s. Over the years, Wally has earned every type of flight certification that's offered. She has trained thousands of people to fly and is considered a legend among female aviators. In 1965, at age 26, she was selected as one of the Outstanding Women in America, and in 2017, her name was inscribed on the Smithsonian National Air & Space Museum's Wall of Honor.

To add to all of this, she is an expert marksman, an antique car enthusiast, and an avid zipliner. She toured Europe and Africa by herself in a VW van and rode elephants, giraffes, and crocodiles. She's won air racing competitions and has accumulated more than 19,500 flight hours.

And yet, for sixty years, she had a dream that was unfulfilled.

At 22, Wally joined a privately-run program to prepare women to fly in space. This ignited her dream to be an astronaut. The testing was relentless, but her experience as an acrobatic pilot and her I-can-do-anything attitude served her well. On one test, spending time in a sensory deprivation tank, she lasted far longer than anyone else — more than 10 hours — beating famed astronaut John Glenn among others. She was primed, ready, and excited to go, and then they shut down the women's program.

She kept alive her dream of going into space, despite so many rejections and roadblocks. She applied to NASA three times, only to be turned away for not having an engineering degree or not having been a test pilot — which was impossible, since the Air Force didn't allow women to fly in those days. It was sexism at it's worst in the 1960s, capped by John Glenn testifying before Congress that "Women pilots go against our social order."

By the time NASA allowed women into the space program, Wally was considered too old. But that didn't kill her dream. Decades later, when Richard Branson announced the Virgin Galatic space program, Wally paid $200,000 to reserve a ticket for one of the flights.

Sixty years is a long time to keep a dream alive, but Wally would've carried this dream to her grave if she'd had to. And then, in July 2021, Amazon founder Jeff Bezos came knocking, inviting Wally to join him and two other people on the first commercial flight of his Blue Origin spacecraft. At age 82, she finally realized her dream.

The flight only lasted eleven minutes, but Wally earned her astronaut's wings. As she said afterwards, "I loved every minute of it. I want to go again. Fast!"

[The second commercial Blue Origin space flight, a few months later, included . . . William Shatner. He does not want to go again.]

What can we learn from these stories? That you can make an impact on people's lives in a lot of different ways. And, while it's not always fun, it's definitely rewarding. We've seen that there is no set formula to becoming a badass; each person reached that peak in their own fashion. What is common to all seven people above are drive, resilience, boldness, unwavering commitment, and joy. These, too, cannot be taught or invoked at will, but are obvious in your rearview mirror.

And that's good. Badassness would be cheapened if it could be acquired by anyone with a wad of cash. Instead, it's a marker or sign that you've put in a lot of work, suffered at times, achieved things that few others have, and you're having an impact on the world. And that, in the long run, is priceless. It means you have been living full out and making the most of this one, precious life you've been given.

Most of these stories do not derive from work-related efforts. That means badassness is open to all, at any age, if you've found something compelling to do and are willing to put in the effort required to create something special. It may be that, like Eddy Goldfarb, you just keep doing until your last breath what you've always loved to do.

Or like Opal Lee, Olga Kotelko, and Shirley Curry, you start from where you are, follow that spark of interest, keep at it, live fully in the moment, and eventually hear, "Wow, what a badass!" As far as legacies go, I can't imagine a better one.

What are your biggest takeaways from this chapter?

Summary (Part 1)

Here are a few simple truths we've covered so far:

- You're only old if you tell yourself you are.
- There is no age limit to doing or starting new things.
- From simple beginnings can come fantastic feats.
- You can add years to your life or throw them away.
- Focus on your health, fitness, mindset, and relationships.
- Having a purpose in life matters a lot to your longevity.
- You don't have to buy into ageist messages.
- You are not a failure if you don't retire.

Your future is completely in your hands, and in your mindset. Don't back off or think your time has passed. You can still do fun, fascinating, even magical things at any age. Your only limits are the ones you accept.

If you started this book wanting a traditional, never-work-again retirement, put a bookmark here. Make any changes to your life that add to your longevity, and then go have a blast. But remember where you put this book. Someday, you may need the second part to help you figure out "What do I do now?"

Meanwhile, if you've been all-in on reinventing yourself, buckle up! Now that we've laid the groundwork for how to live a long, healthy life, let's fill it up with something awesome.

Reinventing Yourself

*You are under no obligation to remain
the same person you were a year ago,
a month ago, or even a day ago.
You are here to create yourself, continuously.*

· Richard Feynman ·

Taking Stock

Okay, I promised you something awesome for your next chapter, right? And why not? You've got one life, you *should* be doing awesome things. That doesn't guarantee you'll be giving speeches at the UN, hanging with the Dalai Lama, and being featured on the covers of prestigious magazines (though that's possible). "Awesome" could be as simple as creating new hiking trails in a nearby state park or writing a book or launching a YouTube channel on the most curious insects you've found. Anything that has you leaping out of bed in the morning to begin working on it and that pings your brain with new ideas at odd hours — *that* puts you in the Land of Awesome, because you'll be feeling so alive and engaged. It's a rare state to be in, and this part of the book will help you get there.

Of course, you have to do the work. I can't magically zap you via these pages and *poof* you're in Awesomeland. But the steps are all here. If you follow them, if you go deep inside yourself, and if you are patient with the process, you can get there.

Patience is critical; there's no way to rush this. The process is the same for everyone, though your journey will be unique to you. Some parts will be fast and easy and some will be challenging, but by staying committed to your big goal, you'll achieve it.

How you look at this process will affect how successful is your journey. If you think it's going to be HARD, it will be. If you think it will be EASY, you won't be prepared when the road takes a sudden turn and you get bounced around. But if you approach this with an open mind, ready for whatever may come up, you'll be much more resilient as the journey unfolds, and you're likely to enjoy the ride.

The major steps in the process are:

Taking Stock

This explores where you are at the moment, where you've been, and what might affect your journey. This is also where you'll work on anything from the past that has its hooks in you. The more you put aside things that are holding you back and silence the limiting stories you're telling yourself, the better prepared you'll be for charging ahead.

Choosing Your New Path

This is where you'll get creative about what your future could look like. You'll dig into not just "What would I like to do?", but also "What *could* I do?" Having a no-limits mindset here can open up unimagined possibilities. By the end of this chapter, you'll have a clear idea of what's next for you.

Launching Your Next Chapter

Now it's time to plot out and launch your journey. In this chapter, you'll get clear on your priorities, focus on the small steps that will really get you going, set up a routine to solidify your commitment, and find ways to help you gain momentum.

Embracing the Struggle

Any worthwhile journey takes time, which opens the door for hurdles, set-backs, and doubt. In this chapter, you'll look at things that might be getting in your way and apply strategies to keep the path — and your head and heart — as clear and focused as possible.

Making It Last

You're not going for a finish line, you're going for a new direction for your life. It will take consistent effort and courage to get there, and this chapter is where you'll lock things in and reap the rewards of all the work you've done.

With the big picture of the journey set, let's dig into where and who you are before charging toward the future; it's like defining "You are here" on the map of your life. This chapter covers five areas and a collection of subtopics. The links between them may not be obvious at first, but they'll all come into play before the end. So . . .

1. Where Are You Right Now?
2. What Are You Saying Goodbye To?
3. What Don't You Want to Regret?
4. What Could Hold You Back?
5. How Committed Are You?

In doing this work, allow yourself to not have immediate answers and don't push away whatever bubbles up in your head. Much of your wisdom lies outside the range of your conscious thoughts, so when something does push through, trust that it's worth examining.

As you go along, pay attention to how you're feeling. Your emotional state affects how you approach the work, how open or closed you are to change and new ideas, and how strong is your commitment to your future, particularly when the road gets rough. That doesn't mean you have to be happy and cheery all the time, but noticing when you're feeling stressed, for example, could prompt you to stop and look more closely into what's going on in that experience. This enables you to correct your course sooner. Knowledge is power, and awareness of your feelings is a valuable tool.

With all that said, let's jump in.

1. Where Are You Right Now?

Do you know this saying: Ready - Fire - Aim? We're not going to do that. You might *feel* like jumping ahead — I've often done that myself (rarely to good effect) — but we're talking about a new direction for your life, so let's establish the baseline of where you are, who you are, and what you really need. This makes the later steps easier, because you'll be clear on some foundational matters.

There's a lot to unpack here, but we'll start with these questions and debrief them below. There are no wrong answers, so be candid in your responses.

Your intentions re: retiring — Full, Partial, Never, or Unsure?

What date, if any, have you set for making this change?

Do you have specific plans for your life with this change?

Who is affected by the change you want to make?

What's the financial impact, if any, of making this change?

Intentions

What you want to do is completely up to you, and it will probably change over time. But being as clear as you can be about your *intentions* regarding a major change in your life, rather than just leaving your ideas in some vague, muddy soup in your brain, gives you more control about when, where, how, and so on. That's why it's so important to write out your answer, even if it's "Haven't got a clue."

Date

If you haven't already retired, do you know when you want to make this change (whether you call it "Retirement," "My next big thing," or "Never")? If you have a date or age in mind, that's great. This allows you to organize your plans and expectations.

If you haven't picked a date and you're nearing an age when most people leave their job, that uncertainty could cause you stress; it has for some of my clients. So picking a date, any date, allows you to take that off your mind; you can always change it later if you need to.

If this life change is five years or more away, good for you for thinking about it now. Pick a date or an age for when you'll do it and then move on. It could even be aspirational and motivate you to prepare for this big inflection point in your life. And it may allow you to brush off things that would otherwise annoy you because, hey, you're not going to have to deal with that BS too much longer.

If you've already retired, but are wondering what to do now, that date is today!

Plans

What plans, if any, have you already made with regard to this next big time in your life? Are you looking to start a business? Maybe take two years to travel the world? Are you so anxious to be freed from work that your plan is to *not* plan anything for at least five years and maybe forever? Or do you have no idea what's next?

As mentioned above, there are no wrong answers. Whatever you have planned so far could be wonderfully fulfilling, or you may find it isn't enough and you want something different in your future.

Two things matter here:

» If you've planned *something*, we want to capture that and can then build from it.

» How much stimulation — mental, physical, and emotional — is built into your plans? Research has shown that people in retirement underestimate how much stimulation they need.

Others

Who will be affected by this change in your life? A spouse or partner? Your children and perhaps grandchildren, if you have them? Friends? Business associates? Your collection of doctors, dentists, and other providers?

I'm not suggesting you should base any of your decisions on the people around you; first and foremost, it has to satisfy you. But it's also rather ostrich-y to presume no one will be affected, or that others' reactions won't impact you. They will. So being specific now about who will be affected helps in your planning. (I only included doctors, dentists, and such because, if you go traveling for a long time, it would be wise to sort out local replacements before you need them.)

Finances

How prepared are you financially for the next phase of your life? Do you have enough money set aside to support you for as long as you live, regardless of what you decide to do with your time? Will you need to supplement the holdings you have in order to do what you really want to do? Do you need to stay employed in order to keep health insurance benefits? Or do you have very little set aside and just need to keep working as long as you can — but still want to have *something* resembling retirement?

There are no judgments or expectations here. Your situation is what it is. But being clear about where you stand financially is a critical factor in deciding on options for the next part of your life.

Who Are You Anyway?

If you've been in a career for a long time, it has shaped your thinking about who you are in the world. If you've been, say, an executive for 30 years, that's likely how you see yourself. You certainly have other labels that may apply, like parent or skier or musician, but one's career is typically the foundation for how most people think of themselves.

So what do you do when that role no longer applies? What if you no longer belong to a club you've been a part of for a very long time?

Being the guest of honor at a retirement party might be a nice send-off, but what happens after that?

The blow of being out of that old role is softened when you've been in control of the process and consciously decided to leave. And it may not feel like a blow at all if you've been longing for the day when you'll be free of working. But don't kid yourself, you're going to feel that change eventually. As one woman lamented, "What do I put on a business card now?"

So ask yourself what is important about how you define yourself, and by extension how you present yourself to the world? What stories do you want to hang onto about your accomplishments, status, money, or whatever? Conversely, what can you let go of regarding how you've defined yourself in the past? If you've been a serial entrepreneur with multiple, highly successful exits, can you see yourself helping out at a non-profit with a fraction of the resources you used to have and let that be your story now? If you've been a doctor, are you okay with being, say, a carpenter, with no need to reach back to "I used to be a doctor..."?

There's no judgment here. If you need validation by others for who you've been or what you've accomplished, being clear about that helps you organize your plans for the future.

But watch out for what Adam Grant, in his book *Think Again,* calls "identity foreclosure." This is the concept that once you've established an identity for yourself, you're done — that is what you'll always be, and the only thing you'll ever be. It doesn't have to be that way, of course. You are not obligated to be only one thing in your life nor to *mention* it, even if you pursued one path for thirty years or more.

What's critical is knowing how far you can stretch in considering new things for your life and how much you can let go of. The wider the playing field, the greater the possibilities for finding something for the future that will absolutely captivate you.

How do you define yourself now?

What About Your Routines?

We all get into routines for how we go through the day, from when we start the coffee to when we head out the door to . . . (so many other parts of our day). We are creatures of habit.

So what happens when some long-held routines end and you're suddenly swamped with possibilities of what you could do? Science has shown that too much choice is worse than none at all. That applies to how you go through the day as much as it does to decisions you have to make about jobs or money or even vacations.

For many people, this becomes completely disorienting. What was familiar and supporting as they went through the day is now gone, leaving them temporarily paralyzed. In trying to find a rhythm, they often tinker with the delicate balance of life at home or with friends. This impacts a lot of people, and a lot of relationships, when someone suddenly retires.

You've probably heard the stories, like the husband who retires and is suddenly around the house all the time, creating projects for himself like rearranging the cupboards that his wife set in place decades before. Or the guy who was so locked into his routine of going to work that, after retiring, he would sit on a bench near his old office to watch his former colleagues eat lunch. There are *lots* of stories like this.

To add to the dog pile of "This is changed and that is changed and this other thing is changed!" are shifts around spending and finances. If you've got a financial plan for retirement, you're already aware of that. It still bears repeating, though, that you need to pay attention to what happens when your financial situation changes *and* you have a lot more time to spend money. Stay vigilant, please.

As for structuring your day when you're released from your old routines, it's important to develop new routines. We'll get into those in greater depth later, but starting today, make reading this book and doing the exercises part of your routine.

What are the daily routines you're likely to miss the most?

What Do You Really Need?

This question might seem fast and easy. It's not. Leaving aside basics, like food, water, sunlight, shelter, companions, and sex, what do you really need — what's the bare minimum you need — to be able to live a life you enjoy?

Don't jump to quick answers. This isn't just a matter of defining your monthly cost of living. It's about what you absolutely must have in money, location, and community.

Getting specific about your needs defines the boundaries of what's possible for you. If your requirements are specific and firm, you will limit the choices available to you for the future. Conversely, if your needs are flexible or small, you greatly expand the range of ideas you can consider.

You may encounter tradeoffs as you think through what you really need. I know a guy who spends $1000 a month on wine; that's part of what makes life special for him. But with that kind of budget, not to mention two mortgages and college tuition, he needs to make enough money to support that lifestyle. If he suddenly decided he wanted to spend a year meditating in Bhutan, chances are he would have to adjust his choices in wine.

Some tradeoffs will be easy, others will be hard; don't sidestep the hard ones. And realize that in some cases, such as where you live, being flexible on your choices pays huge dividends.

Here's an example. I have lived in Boulder, Colorado for over 20 years. This is an awesome town and I feel blessed to be here. We have great friends, we raised our kids here, and I could see spending the rest of my life in Boulder. But if I came up with a new direction for my life that required me to move, either because the opportunity was elsewhere or because I had to reduce my living expenses, I would do that in a heartbeat. At least for me, what I'm doing and how it feeds my soul are infinitely more important than where I'm doing it. (Hey, wife, you agree with that, right? Right?)

My little aside brings up an important point. You will probably not be making such significant decisions in a vacuum. Other people are likely to be affected by your decisions, including about the baseline needs for your life, so be sure to include them in your assessments.

The exercise below has three parts to it. Here are the contexts:

- *How much, or little, money do you need to live and support your family?* This isn't the time to load up on wishes, hopes, and dreams; what's the minimum amount you need to get by? You don't have to get really rigorous about this unless that's how you're wired; a rough calculation, say on a monthly basis, should be sufficient.

- *Where do you absolutely have to live, both in domicile and location?* Could you downsize if you needed to, have you been planning on buying something new, or do you want to stay where you are? It's important to be clear on what's non-negotiable and what's flexible. This goes for city and country, too.

■ *What do your relationships and community need to include?* Interaction with other people is critical to life. So, how engaged do you need to be with other people? Are you part of a spiritual community? Do you have family scattered around the country whom you need to visit regularly? Do you have a weekly poker game that you just can't give up? What are the must-haves in your involvement with others?

What are your must-haves re: MONEY?

What are your must-haves re: LOCATION?

What are your must-haves re: RELATIONSHIPS?

2. What Are You Saying Goodbye To?

You have a transition ahead of you — the end of one thing, a period of resetting, and the start of something new. And along the way, you'll need to give up some things.

That sounds simple and academic, doesn't it? The actual process is anything but that. It is often fraught with uncertainty, disorientation, and a feeling of loss before you get centered again and charge off in a new direction. Everyone is different, of course, so how you experience this phase will be unique to you. It could be fairly fast and smooth, or it could be long, drawn out, and emotional. Be open for anything and, if you can, be curious about how you're reacting.

What is important is acknowledging that one phase of your life is coming to an end, and with that comes the need to say goodbye to things. You are not physically dying when you finish your working career, but there is a figurative death of a chunk of life as you've known it. You won't go back into the office, your work email accounts and phone number will be terminated, you won't get that regular paycheck you had been getting, and so on. A certain way of life for you is or will be gone. Even if you're joyful about this transition, there is still some loss you'll experience. And if you were laid off or otherwise pushed out, you already know the sting of this death.

Grieving is okay, even necessary. Don't short-change this or order yourself to get over it. Take as much time as you need. But pay attention, too; the longer you grieve, the more you postpone what's coming next. The most important thing is just to acknowledge this step. If you try to bury those thoughts about what has ended, they'll hang around and jump up to bite you from time to time, through confusion, doubt, disconnecting from the present, or uncertainty about what you've moved into.

One way to free yourself for new growth is to have a ceremony or ritual to celebrate all that you've done before; that both acknowledges your earlier life and puts an endpoint on it. Until you close that loop, it will be hard to redirect your energies for whatever is to come. Honor the past and thank it for all it has given you, then turn to the future.

How you memorialize this time in your life is up to you. You could have a big, blowout party. You could go off on a week-long retreat to ponder the richness and the struggles you experienced in that job or career. Or you might just go for a walk and release to the winds all that you experienced before.

Of course, if you're still in a job, you probably don't want to celebrate yet. You can, however, *plan* the party, ceremony, or retreat for when you'll cross that threshold. Just keep in mind that this is a step you need to take.

What are the hardest things for you to say goodbye to?

How will you celebrate the chapter that's ending?

3. What Don't You Want to Regret?

"That's a car?!"

My nine-year-old self was transfixed by photos of the just-released 1963 Corvette Stingray. It had sharp, flowing lines and these amazing headlights that flipped up out of the steeply raked front end. It looked like a space ship.

In that moment was born a dream of having a car-of-the-future. For the first 50 years of the dream, I wanted a Corvette. Then I discovered the Tesla Model S and again uttered those immortal words: "That's a car?!"

My dream shifted from Corvette to Tesla, but it never wavered. There have been few things in my life that I really, really wanted; a car-of-the-future was one of them. Seriously, almost every day for 56 years, I would get a little pang of desire. And once (pre-Tesla obsession), when I was swooning over a beautiful Corvette, my wife said, "Oh, go ahead and buy one." I even got her to sign a piece of paper confirming her consent.

But I didn't rush out and buy a Corvette. There were always things in the way — two kids approaching college, job changes, mortgage payments, the possibility of having to support aging parents, and so on. I would sigh when I would see one of my dream cars and think, "Some day..."

Meanwhile, I ended up becoming a coach and worked to help my clients attain *their* dreams. One day, a thought burst into my head — *How can I advocate for my clients to strive for their dreams if I can't do that for myself?*

Oof. I had no good answer. Meanwhile, a lot of the things that had earlier been smart reasons for not taking a leap into my dream had been resolved. Even on the money front, some of my investments had done extremely well in the market, so I actually had some money to play with.

The dream started calling to me *loudly*. And with the release of the Tesla Model 3, at almost half the cost of the other Teslas, it seemed kind of affordable. (I know that's a relative term.)

The one major hurdle was my wife. Even though I had that years-old paper with her signature saying I could buy the car of my dreams, I knew she would be PISSED if I actually did it. She was not into cars.

Back inside *my* head, this thought took hold:

When I get to the end of my life, I don't want to regret not having realized my dream.

So I did it. I put down a deposit and went home to talk with my wife. To say she was furious would be an understatement. I, however, was resolute. I had committed to realizing my dream, to not leaving a big regret out there, and nothing was going to deter me. I survived that first conversation and several subsequent ones, and I got the car. I had realized my dream!

And, you know what, it was totally worth it. I've had the car for three years and I still say "Thank you!" to the heavens every time I drive it. It really is a car-of-the-future. As for my wife, she is now infatuated with it and drives it every chance she gets.

This story is not to point at *things* and suggest that's what you should pursue, like Teslas, mansions, or your own private island. Having a car-of-the-future is only part of what I wanted and want for my life. And though that dream stayed with me for 56 YEARS, there is so much else I don't want to regret that you can't slap a price tag on.

Here's why this exercise is so important, whether what you want is a private jet or world peace. By focusing on what you really, really want — what you don't want to *regret* at the end of your life — you add emotion, conviction, and rich future-focused thinking to your mindset. Putting your mind into that kind of space helps expand your range of possibilities. It helps you think way out of the box and way beyond the Land of No Regrets. You switch from thinking "How can I possibly get there?" to "How can I make this happen?" That is an incredibly potent (and, dare I say, sexy) place for your mind to be! You leap past limitations and small thinking to the realm of Yes! Yes! Yes! (Oof, it's getting warm in here . . .)

Now, some people may think, "I don't want to change the world, John. I'd like to have <my No-Regrets desire>, but otherwise my life is pretty good." That's cool. I get it. AND I'm sure there's more out there that can grab you, fire you up, and fill you with joy. So stay open to the possibility of something developing for you that is beyond what you've ever imagined. Being aware of and acting on what you don't want to regret in your life are excellent ways to open up your thinking.

What do you not want to regret at the end of your days?

4. What Could Hold You Back?

You can have anything you want as long as
you give up the belief that you can't have it.
· Dr. Robert Anthony ·

In a perfect world, I could leave that quote here as a reminder, you'd go "Yep. Got it.", and we'd move on to the next chapter right away.

This, however, is not a perfect world. So despite the wisdom in that quote, we need to talk about things that can hold you back, things that limit you, derail you, or even keep you from starting in the first place. It all revolves around the stories you're telling yourself — stories about how to act, what you can reach for, your relationship to fear, and more. Examining these stories is important for everyone; I've overcome lots of stories that don't serve me, but I still get bitten by ones I haven't resolved or just didn't know were lurking around.

In this section, we'll shine a light on some of the key factors that could limit you and then start working on strategies to resolve them. This is a long-term process, so don't expect immediate results. Just creating awareness gives you the chance to be more in control about how you handle situations. And working through crap is actually a good thing. Not only does it clear away blockages, but it makes you stronger and more resilient.

So, buckle up! The road is about to get bumpy.

I work with some very accomplished people. They've made great, long careers for themselves, as well as a lot of money. On the surface, you would think their life was perfect or pretty damned close to it. What could possibly keep them from making the next phase of their life something fabulous? Plenty, as it turns out.

For some, it's the stories they make up about themselves, stories that limit what they consider is possible going forward. For others, it's being a slave to what got them to where they are, as opposed to being open to *anything.* A common story in this cohort is being too comfortable with life as it is now to really put in the effort to achieve the change they want. Or being fearful about money, even when they have a lot of it. The list could be endless, but we'll tackle six of these below.

There are two main types of impediments to change: 1) not getting started at all, and 2) limiting the range of possibilities for what you might do. The non-starter mode could be a result of fear or doubt or needing everything to be clear before you take a first step. The limiting mode usually comes from looking at your future through the lens of what you've done in the past. Neither of these barriers will help you build a dynamic new direction for your life.

Rules

In recent years, as I've been working on my shit (or, more accurately, on my head and heart), I've come to think of my upbringing as having been guided by a book — an immense, dusty, leather-bound monster, several feet tall and wide and thick, which makes a thunderous sound when you open it, and which contains every rule ever created for how to live.

Want to know how to dress for a date? See page 12,432 in the middle of the left side. Want to know how to react if you're fired? That would be on page 386,212. Want to know whether to buy a puppy or have children or donate to worthy causes? They're all in the book. *Everything* is in the book.

Or so it felt. In unconsciously believing all answers were outside myself, it made me question my own judgment, from age 2 to my early 60s. Not always, of course; I had my radical, Fuck-you-Book! moments. But by default, my thoughts and my behavior were closely aligned with that frickin' book.

The thing is, we all have some form of that book, though hopefully not as massive and directive as mine. The entries in the book are written by our families and society, and it gets updated by how and where we're living, and by what we experience in life. On a daily basis, much of how we act is dictated by that book, even if we don't consciously see ourselves flipping the pages to find the needed guidance.

Vishen Lakhiani, in his wonderful book *The Code of the Extraordinary Mind*, has a term he calls "Brules," which is short for "bullshit rules." And many (most?) of the rules in our lives are just that — bullshit. Brules include things like "boys don't cry," "women are the weaker sex," and so on. Just flat out bullshit that none of us need. Lakhiani recommends, and I heartily second, that you don't have to follow any of those brules if you don't want to.

How do rules apply to reinventing your life? Well, which ones are serving you and which ones are holding you back? Which ones help you navigate tough terrain and which ones say, "Give up and go back to the bar"? If you're not aware of who is driving the proverbial bus — your future self or the brules from your past — it's probably the brules.

As you become aware of the rules you live by, particularly those you'd classify as brules, start making choices. Start saying, "I *won't* actually do that any longer," with "that" being whatever doesn't serve you. Then choose a thought or action that *is* in alignment with a more positive, self-directed you.

And what might some of those brules be? For starters, anything you'd like to say "No" to but have previously done out of a sense of obligation. Here are some examples *(and how to respond):*

- Boring family reunions? *Sorry, can't make it.*
- Making cookies for a school bake sale? *No time; here's $20.*
- Meditating because you think you should? *Nap instead.*
- Going to a business conference you hate? *Send someone else.*

How about things that brules say you shouldn't do?

- Starting a new career in your 60s? *Who says you can't?*
- Going back to school "at your age?" *Hell, yes!*
- Finding a new lover in your 70s or 80s? *Yay, you!*
- Going on a solo trek around the world? *Why not?*

Scrutinizing the brules in your life is not a one-off exercise. You can't just bring a brule into the light and be instantly freed from its tractor beam of compliance. You've had a long time to groove your neurons to obey that brule, so you'll need several occasions of saying "Nope" to something before it's finally under control.

With each brule, ask yourself whether your thoughts are helping you grow or making you conform to someone else's idea of what is right. If the answer is "Conformity," find a different angle that better serves *you*, not the norm.

What are some of the "brules" (bullshit rules) in your life?

Past Success

It's great to be successful, to be lauded for what you've accomplished. And you can keep on rolling down that track if you still feel excited about your work.

If the buzz has worn off, however, or you really want to try something different, then box up those old achievements and set them aside. If you don't cling to what made you successful before, if you allow yourself to approach things with a "beginner's mind" and be messy and clumsy and open to *everything*, you've got a solid chance to create a fabulous new chapter in your life.

The bigger question is how attached are you to being as successful in your new venture as you've been in the past? Do you feel compelled to match your prior achievements, or can you say, "Hey, look at this blank canvas! What can I paint on it?"

You still get to use all your wisdom and capabilities, but when you can say, "What shall I build now?" instead of "I have to keep doing what I've done" or "I have to be as successful as before" then you're free to see what is truly possible for you.

A related question is "Who is keeping score?" When you care about what others think — or what you *imagine* they're thinking — that puts the focus outside yourself and invites in that pesky ego that needs to be fed, to be loved, to be *seen*.

How would it be to approach this new You without attachment to how you're being perceived by others? Can you do things for the sake of doing them, to do things for the joy of doing them, to do things because they light you up inside — and only because of that?

If you do things that inspire you, chances are high that others will notice. There's something really compelling about people who are in flow and living fully and authentically. There's something magical and magnetic about them. So go for *that*, please, not for the applause. Be fully yourself, doing whatever it is that you really want to do, and you'll be wonderful. (And probably applauded as well, but who's counting?)

What's important about your past successes?

Playing It Safe

If you need to see the future clearly before you take your first step toward it, you won't get far. If you need guarantees and certainty, decide when you'll start getting your Social Security checks and forget about the rest.

That may sound harsh, but there's no gentle way to say it. Trying to create a compelling new future is inherently uncertain. If you've been in one line of work for most of your life, trying to navigate the uncertainty of "What now?" can feel particularly daunting.

Dealing with life is dealing with uncertainty. From simple things like what will you have for dinner to more weighty things like "What if our kid doesn't get into college?" to really serious questions like "Should I have that surgery or not?" or "When do we put our dear, aged dog down?"

Deciding about a new direction for your life, however, carries its own, elevated level of uncertainty, particularly because the choices you make will have a ripple effect on every other part of your life, as well as the lives of people around you.

In the face of that, many people play it safe. They make choices that don't push them too far or too hard. Intentionally choosing something risky is frightening to a lot of people. But playing it safe means you're playing small. And playing small is a huge waste of the big, wonderful life you've been given. Do you really want to live the rest of your days being less than you can be?

Mark Zuckerberg, CEO of Facebook, said this about uncertainty and its companion, risk:

"The biggest risk is not taking any risk . . . In a world that is changing really quickly, the only strategy that is guaranteed to fail is not taking risks."

What he's talking about is embracing uncertainty and stepping boldly forward even when you can't see a clear path to the end goal you seek. But you know what? You are resourceful and resilient and can figure this shit out.

Even if life doesn't feel wonderful right now or uncertainty about the future seems overwhelming, the potential for a truly meaningful life is always there.

As for overcoming a desire for certainty, start with awareness of how you're feeling about this change, make a commitment to not playing small, and remind yourself of this commitment every time a part of you wants to pull back to the land of safety and certainty. Keep choosing change, and keep choosing you.

What's your tolerance for risk?

"What If?"

This is a companion to playing it safe. Indulging in a game of "What If" makes it easier to retreat to a safe approach, particularly when the road ahead looks bumpy or unclear. Here are some examples:

- What if I'm not successful?
- What if I don't make any money at this?
- What if others don't approve, or they ridicule or shun me?
- What if I get into this and then find that I don't like it?
- What if this requires changes in other parts of my life?
- What if this is a step down from what I've done before?

When it comes to charting a new future for yourself, you need to be on the lookout for thoughts like these that can short-circuit your efforts. It would be tragic to hold yourself back just because you're stuck in a What If loop.

The question is how do you want to be with your What Ifs? Do you want to let them run your decisions or do you want to use them as catapults to get you further?

I'm not suggesting you say "Fuck 'em all!" and dash headlong into *whatever* lies ahead; a certain measure of caution, or at least attention, is useful. If you're on the edge of a swamp in Florida, it's a good idea to scan for alligators — but the possible presence of alligators is no reason not to be there.

Here's how to turn things around. Make a list of **Stories I'm Telling Myself.** Stories lurk in every What If you have, so it's time to bring them out into the light. If you were doing this exercise with the What Ifs above, those stories would look like this:

- I will never be successful.
- I can't make money.
- Other people don't approve of me.
- I'm afraid of being trapped in something I don't want to do.
- I'm scared of change.
- It's humiliating to do something less than I've done before.

Oof. It hurts tapping into those feelings. AND YET . . . We all have lists like that. We have a collection of stories that hold us back, make us question ourselves, or drive us into decisions or behaviors that aren't in our best interest.

I asked one very brave client to make a list of the stories she was telling herself, and she came back with 55 items! She dug deeper than anyone I've ever seen. Does that mean she's more messed up than others? Not at all. She just got brutally honest with herself and kept letting the stories roll out. That showed tremendous courage.

The true power of listing your stories is that you will see your life with new clarity and then can work on the things that will give you the greatest benefits. This is hard, even painful work, but it is ultimately liberating. And a liberated you is a you who can scale unimagined heights.

What limiting stories are you telling yourself?

Money

This is another area that can get quite problematic. Rules/brules, past success, playing safe, and What Ifs all contribute to money concerns that can keep you up at night — even if you have a lot of money. And if you don't have buckets of money stashed away and can't afford to retire, this topic becomes even more charged and emotional.

What's a person to do?

If you have a financial planner or some other professional to help you navigate these waters, good for you. If you don't have one, consider getting one, or at least check out the many books, blogs, and podcasts for direction.

What we *can* look at right now is this: Are you living to make money or making money to live?

That may not be an easy question to answer. Yes, money is important to have, particularly if you're planning, at some point, to never work again. But are money considerations driving your decisions, or are they lower on your list of concerns? Do your accomplishments get passed through a filter of how much money they earned, as though that's the final arbiter of value? I don't ask that with any judgment; I know several people for whom that's true.

If you don't have enough money set aside, or you have enough to live on but not to take a 30-year vacation, then of course money needs to be in the top tier of considerations.

But I've found that many people base their decisions on some archaic brules about how much money they should have to live, even when they have more than they need. It's like an artificial scarcity mentality.

There's an exercise below for you to write out any concerns you may have about money in your future. Once you've done that, I ask you to park those thoughts as you go through the rest of this book. If you're going to create something awesome in your future, you may limit yourself by making money your first (and only?) filter.

Give yourself the freedom to explore what's possible for you, without restriction or testing it against some economic model. Just let your ideas flow, and maybe even soar; don't shoot them down before they've had a chance to fill you with ideas and options and intrigue. Take this time for YOU. You can always invoke the banker's presence at some point.

I don't give you this invitation flippantly. Eventually, you will need to give your most potent ideas a reality check. But if you've got something that absolutely captivates you, something that has given you a sense of *mission*, you will find a way to make it work.

What are your concerns about money?

Fear

This has been lurking in every one of the topics above.

- For RULES, there's the fear of not being compliant with the rules/brules and thus being judged or rejected.

- For PAST SUCCESS, the fear is of not measuring up to some standard or level of achievement you've reached before (and thus what has become of you?!).

- For PLAYING IT SAFE and WHAT IFs, there's the fear of *not* being safe, and what that would mean if all those horrible What If disasters actually happened?

- For MONEY, fear of destitution or heavy debts can be debilitating.

Fear is tricky. It doesn't *feel* like it's a good thing, but fear is often a sign that there's something you need to pay attention to. The fact that you're feeling fear, however — or something you *call* fear — doesn't mean that whatever it's trying to warn you about is wrong or bad; it may just be something you need to focus on and perhaps act upon. As Marie Forleo says in her wonderful book, *Everything is Figureoutable,* "Fear is not the enemy." (Mic drop)

I had a major insight about fear during my acting years in New York. Being an introvert, it was tough facing fear and rejection multiple times a week as I went to auditions. It never seemed to get better while I waited for my turn, though I got through it each time once I was in the midst of the audition.

Then one day it dawned on me — I wasn't nervous and fearful at all. The pounding heart and sweaty palms weren't a sign that I was about to fail, it was just my body getting amped up to perform! That realization changed everything for me.

If you've ever seen drag racers waiting to start, they rev their engines to the max as the lights go from red to yellow to green. When the light hits green, they race off at full power. Your body does the same thing when you have to present yourself in some way, whether that's at a business meeting, a stage performance, or on a first date. Your body wants you to be sharp, focused, and "on" when it's your turn, so it gets you ready in advance.

Unfortunately, most people interpret that as fear, which can lead to doubt and visions of failure locking up both your mind and your body. I did that, too, until I understood that my body — not my brain — was doing *exactly* what it was supposed to do.

Granted, it's a weird state to be in, smiling and confident, while your body is churning. But knowing that you're feeling what you're supposed to feel should help you reorient your mind and stay focused on what you want to achieve, rather than trying to "get the butterflies in your stomach to fly in formation."

Even if your fear scenario isn't about being in the spotlight, and you're convinced it's out and out fear, you don't have to be ruled by it. You can start to pick it apart as noted above, or you can ask yourself, "What's the worst thing that could happen?"

There's a great exercise you can do if you sense that fear could derail your efforts to create an awesome new chapter in your life. I was introduced to this in Adam Markel's book *Pivot*. He calls this your "fear story." To do it, write down what it is you really fear, in all its horrible glory and to its ultimate, inevitable, calamitous conclusion. Make it as rich and catastrophic as you can. Then put it aside for a little bit. When you come back to read how disastrous your life could be, you're bound to see how "unlikely, exaggerated, and in many cases almost comical" is your fear story (as described by Markel). At that point, you can decide if you really want to stay locked into that story or create a new, more positive and forward-going story.

I suggest you choose the positive, forward-going path.

Write out your fear story. (Make it juicy!)

5. How Committed Are You?

Weight training could easily be seen as a form of masochism. It's not just about pushing yourself, repeatedly, to a point of pain and failure. (Okay, muscular failure, but failure nonetheless.) It's also about *choosing* to be uncomfortable in the present moment for a longer term gain.

I think about that three times a week, when I'm struggling to eke out a few more reps of a weight that is at the edge of what I can handle. I *know* it's going to hurt, yet I continue to do the work.

Why? Because every tough set, every just-one-more rep, adds another day to my existence and improves the quality of my life decades from now. You may call that mental gymnastics, but it definitely helps me get through a workout when there are loud voices in my head shouting, "Enough!" Doing this work is a commitment to having a vital life to the end of my days and I am willing to suffer for it.

How about you? What are you willing to suffer for?

When you have a strong commitment to something deep and elemental in your life, you will summon untold energies and creativity to support your work. You don't have to have a go-ahead-and-beat-me-up kind of mentality to do this, but lacking a true, unshakable commitment to what you want to achieve could leave you saying, "Well, I *thought* I wanted that, but I guess not."

So, how prepared are you to keep going when the going gets tough? And presuming that your commitment is strong, what will you do at the first sign (and the next and the next) of a rocky road? Here's a way to think about it.

Imagine there's this spectacular mountain in the distance, shining in the sun. Everyone you know says that reaching the summit is a must-do trek. So you start out one morning, full of anticipation, picturing what the views must be like from the top. People have described being at the peak as a religious experience and you're excited to capture that feeling yourself.

For the first part of the journey, you're racing along a smooth, paved path. You hit a rhythm and the miles just fly beneath your feet. Then the path turns to gravel, but it's still pretty flat, so you keep blasting along. You're gaining in elevation, but it still feels rather effortless.

All of a sudden you turn a corner and there are rocks in the way. There are so many of them that you can't just cruise through it; you have to pay attention to every step and watch where you place your feet. You stop for a moment and look up the trail and all you see are more and more rocks, and twists and turns as the path disappears into the trees. You look around and you can't even see that shining pinnacle you've been heading for; it's just a solid wall of trees and a growing sense of darkness.

What do you do now? And why did no one tell you about the rocks? Are they sadists, secretly chuckling about the agony you're going through? Or did you take a wrong turn somewhere? You move forward slowly, and it's becoming a chore. You do get little glimmers of light piercing through the trees, reminding you that the mountain peak is still somewhere up there, but you've lost any sense of timing or even conviction that you actually want to get there.

This is the moment when a lot of people turn back, when they decide that reaching the summit is not something they wanted that badly.

There is a trail very much like this an hour from my home. It leads to a gorgeous mountain lake, surrounded by steep peaks. It starts out with a beautiful walk through the forest, with sunlight dappling the trees and cool breezes flowing over you. You can hear birds chirping and water rushing down a nearby creek.

Midway through the trek, however, is a rock field that's a half-mile long and torturous to get through. Really, all you see are rocks, rocks, rocks, with a wall of trees on either side. I've done this hike four times and, since it's an out-and-back trail, I've gone through that rock field eight times. I've hated that part every time.

But it hasn't kept me from doing this hike. The payoff *is* glorious. And, being a good Coloradan, I don't even wear sturdy hiking boots to get through that nasty section. When you're really focused on the present moment, on just taking the next step, you can do this in sneakers, which is exactly how I've gone through that rock field. (My son says he'd do it in flip-flops. Kids...)

By focusing just on the next step, and the next, you can get through anything, as long as your commitment is strong.

So embrace the discomfort — even welcome it, since it's a sign that you're really making progress. Before you know it, you'll be past the nasty rock field and surging onward again.

From 1-10, how strong is your commitment to this effort?

If it's less than a 10, what would make it a 10?

About Pausing on the Trail

Sometimes, in the midst of a rocky patch, you might feel like taking a break. That's okay if you're feeling beaten down by the effort; recovery is important. But if you get too comfortable in that break, or you're resisting what's up ahead, you'll find it harder and harder to get restarted. Don't shy away from the effort or discomfort. Keep choosing your future.

Moving Ahead

By now, you should have a firm view of where you are at the moment and what really matters to you. If you skipped any of the exercises, go back and do them. Getting grounded now is so important for what follows. This whole thing about grappling with transitions and new identities and brules and fears — it like a hornet's nest you're dealing with.

So be patient, take the time to really get solid on who you are at your core, plus what can help you and what can hold you back, and enter the next phase with clear eyes and a committed heart. You owe it to your future self.

What are your three biggest takeaways from this chapter?

What can you put into action TODAY?

Choosing Your New Path

Life isn't about finding yourself.
It's about creating yourself.
· George Bernard Shaw ·

At one point when I first lived in New York City, I had an apartment in an out-of-the way section of Brooklyn. It's now hipster heaven, but at the time it was a collection of leftover shops and run-down apartment buildings, vestiges of a better time when the factories nearby hummed with activity.

My landlady owned the neighborhood candy shop and had spent almost her entire life within a five-mile radius of her home. I was floored to learn she had never been west of New York City — and had no interest in venturing outside her bubble.

"Why should I go anywhere else?" she said. "I have everything I need right here. I have family, food, my social circle. If I want a change of scenery, I can go to Rockaway Beach."

I rattled off activities and places outside the five boroughs of New York, things too wonderful not to be experienced, but she was resolute. "Nope, I'm comfortable where I am," she said.

A year later, a friend talked her into going on a cruise, departing from Miami. When she returned, she was bursting with excitement at this new adventure and told me she was going to make up for lost time in experiencing more of the world.

That's where we are right now. You have a chance to explore new realms, but are you willing to leave the comfortable bubble of the things you've known, the things you've believed about yourself, and how you've imagined your future? This chapter is an invitation to do just that. We're not going to jump into a list of three things you might want to do and then compare pros and cons for each. We're talking about going waaaaay outside the proverbial box and waaaaay beyond what you've ever imagined for yourself, then progressively narrowing things down until you have the one thing that sets your heart ablaze.

The good news is that letting your thoughts and ideas loose costs you nothing. You can be as expansive as possible and no one will know about it unless you tell them, so don't hold back! You'll find a lot of exercises in this chapter to help you in the process, so take the time to work through them.

Here's where we're going in this chapter:

1. Priming Your Brain
2. Goals, Purpose, and Passion
3. Deep Dive on What's Next
4. Ignite Your Thinking
5. It's Time to Choose

1. Priming Your Brain

You have deep thinking ahead of you. Whether that puts a smile on your face or a trace of tension, it's the only way you're going to develop a direction for your future that can inspire and sustain you for years. There is no button to press that provides instant results.

We can make the process easier and more fruitful by tapping into neuroscience. Researchers have found that your state of mind affects how open and expansive is your thinking. If you're in an upbeat frame of mind, activating your "positive emotional attractors" (PEA), you'll develop a wider range of ideas and insights than if you'd activated your "negative emotional attractors" (NEA, which includes the fight-flight-

or-freeze impulse). Another way to think about this is that you can prime your brain to be more creative.

That may seem obvious, but have you ever intentionally shifted your mood before going into deep thinking or decision-making mode? I'm a really creative guy, but I rarely made an explicit effort to prime my brain until I learned about this.

Where you do this work also affects whether your PEA or your NEA is activated. Process-oriented places, like your office or your kitchen may not be ideal for doing these exercises. Activities where you narrow your focus can put clamps on your brain at a time when you want it to fly freely.

Here are some ideas of places and things that can help you open up your PEA and get your creative juices really flowing:

- Find some upbeat music that gets you going. Or do some light exercise, dancing, or shadow boxing, anything to get your heart rate elevated.

- Do random doodling for a few minutes, if sketching is your jam.

- Watch some funny videos on YouTube.

- Go for a walk — around the block, in the hills, on a beach, or wherever you can find that shifts your brain out of "work" mode and into "create."

- Go to a park to do this discovery work, or a coffee shop or the library, anywhere other than where you do most of your work at home or the office.

- Lie on your bed or the floor, just to change your perspective.

You can combine these or create your own pre-flight program. My go-to combo, as I'm waiting for my computer to start up, is to sing an upbeat song and punch my arms in the air. It's all about establishing a fertile environment to open up your mind, and developing a routine that can quickly get you into a creative state. And don't do this just once, but get yourself pumped up for all these brainstorming sessions. In fact, before you move on to the next section, do something now to activate your PEA.

What will you do to elevate your mood?

2. Goals, Purpose, and Passion

There's a little more foundational work to do, with factors that link to where we're going in this chapter. It's useful to understand some of your basic drivers, and not just what's in your head, but in your heart and your gut as well. We're looking for those things that will pull you forward and keep you going when part of you might want to quit.

Goals

It's hard to get somewhere if you don't know where you're going. Sure, some folks, released from the structure of work, love being aimless — nothing to do, nowhere to go except what you feel like doing in the moment. That joy in unlimited freedom only lasts a few years for most people, however, and then they come to this place of "What am I going to do with my life now?"

Having a goal or vision of what you want to do is important; that's a big part of what we'll be exploring. But goals can have a dark side if you find yourself in a continual hunt, as you reach your next goal and your next, of always chasing *something*. Also, goals can weigh you down if you look at what you want to achieve and find yourself lacking because you haven't reached it yet.

A way to buffer yourself from the shadow side of these *Doing* goals is to have a companion *Being* goal or goals to balance the scale. Then, whether you achieve the measurable results you're striving for or you find yourself in a very different place, these Being goals will keep you feeling like your efforts aren't being wasted.

What are Being goals? They're the ways you want to feel and be and interact with the world as you go through the day. This might seem like woowoo, but at your core, these are the most important goals you can strive for.

Do you want to feel happy to the end of your days? Inspired each morning? Respected? Loved? Grateful? The list could be endless. Life is different when you consciously choose this path, rather than hoping to feel this way as you doggedly pursue some achievement.

And what part of you have you always wished to express, like artistic, entrepreneurial, mobilizing, or adventurous? Most people have something deep inside they've longing to do or be. What if you made *that* your goal?

Being goals are perpetual goals, without a finish line, but with a clear state that allows you to see at any moment if you are in alignment with these goals or not. Take "Inspired" as an example. If this is how you want to feel each day, and you find yourself grumbling along, you can stop and say, "What can I do right now to feel inspired?" And that thing you do could be related to your big *Doing* goal, or it could be something simple, like watching puppy videos, that reminds you there's more to life than whatever is troubling you at the moment. Either way, that conscious shift improves your mood in that moment.

Once you've put a stake in the ground for *how* you want to live your life going forward, you'll make it much easier to achieve *what* you want to do.

How do you want to feel in this next chapter of your life?

What part of you hasn't yet been expressed?

Purpose and Passion

As we covered briefly in the *Optimize Your Life* chapter, having a purpose in life is critical to increasing your health span and longevity. And, that purpose doesn't have to be something grand; it could be as basic as "My purpose is to learn and share something new each day."

At its purest, purpose is a synthesis of everything you are — your talents, desires, fears, passions, and hopes — coupled with a focus that goes beyond just yourself. It's hard to define a singular thing that easily ties up all those aspects.

As well, your purpose (or "Why," mission, or calling) should be something that inspires you to action, not something that you'd put on a billboard to proclaim "This is why I'm here!" It should be as much about how you're being as what you're doing.

So let's change our focus from purpose with a capital "P" to what's at the heart of purpose, which is having something you contribute to the world — something you contribute willingly, passionately, tirelessly. Said another way: What is the impact you want to have on others?

Your purpose comes out of your efforts, what you share, and whom you affect. It's not something that you *find*, despite the 17 billion blog posts on that theme. Instead, it grows from a seed of interest and curiosity into something vibrant and useful and inspiring. Trying to find a purpose is like trying to find happiness — if you go in search of it, you'll probably end up disappointed, but if you follow what fascinates you, it will appear as you're deep into your work.

There's a companion to Purpose that we need to address, which is Passion. You'll hear "Follow your passion" almost as often as "What's your purpose?" Some people like the idea of discovering and following a passion, and some people are intimidated as hell by that. Ultimately, it doesn't matter, because trying to *find* your passion is as vague and fruitless as trying to find your purpose — neither of them are sitting idly on a bench waiting for you to walk by. Nor do either of them strike like a bolt of lightning, where you suddenly go, "Oh, *that's* my purpose/passion!"

Actually, you may have an "Aha" moment about this, but it will be a quiet one, when you're deep into something that started off from a spark of curiosity. If you follow that curiosity long enough, you'll likely realize some day that, "Hey, I really love what I'm doing, and this is meaningful for others as well."

That's a purpose well-lived. So look for things that make you say, "That's interesting," or "Huh…" or that send you down a rabbit hole of curiosity. Then build from there.

What impact do you want to have on others?

What are you really curious about?

135

3. Deep Dive on What's Next

Okay, it's time to dig into what you might pursue for the next chapter of your life. It took us a while to get here, but all that earlier work was needed to clear away the things that might have limited you, diverted you, or slowed you down. If you've done all the work so far, you're ready to go.

We'll start with a brain dump of things you've thought you might do, or wanted to do, or secretly wished you could do — and lots of things you haven't imagined. Of course, you might already have a couple ideas in mind, or maybe you know the one thing you really want to do. If so, that's great, but don't skip over this part. There may be other ways you could approach that one thing, or perhaps that one thing could be a springboard to something even more compelling.

In the box below, write out 20 things you could do, no matter how different some may be from what you've done before. Don't worry about whether you can pull these off, or if they pay enough, or how long it takes to achieve, just see how far you can stretch the limits of what's possible for you.

This isn't about trips you want to take. We're talking consuming, inspiring, *I-love-my-life!* kinds of things. Or quiet little *well-that's-interesting* and boisterous *wouldn't-that-be-fun* ideas; they don't all have to be "Eureka!" moments to qualify. You'll likely come up with five to seven ideas to start, but don't stop there. Pushing yourself to come up with 20 different things takes your brain into rarely-traveled territory.

When I did this, my offbeat ideas included museum curator, dog trainer, cabaret singer, and videographer. Am I likely to do any of those things, let alone all of them? Maybe not. But could I imagine myself in each of those roles and having a fabulous time? Yes, absolutely. The point, right now, is to not go only for practical ideas. It's to explore whatever pops into your brain, no matter how crazy, unrealistic, or surprising it is. You never know when two unlikely options will spark an inspiring — and achievable — new idea.

If you get stuck, here are some ways to prompt new thoughts:

- What did you want to do when you were a kid?
- What do you love most about your current or a past job?
- What bigger thing could a hobby turn into
- What gets you excited? What makes you mad?
- What could you learn from someone you admire?
- What can you draw from answers earlier in this chapter?

The possibilities are only limited by your imagination, so let it rip! As you do this, don't analyze, just write, write, write. To rev this up, set a timer for five minutes and see how many ideas you get in that time. (But do all 20, regardless of how long it takes.)

Ideas About Future Activities

1.	11.
2.	12.
3.	13.
4.	14.
5.	15.
6.	16.
7.	17.
8.	18.
9.	19.
10.	20.

As you look back through your list, which ones stand out? Did any of these surprise you? Which ones have the greatest pull or resonance for you? Have any themes or categories appeared?

The next step in this deep dive is to choose five ideas or categories. You'll take each of these and drill even further down by finding five more possibilities for each one. Here are some examples:

If you chose, say, "writer," some drill-down possibilities could be: novelist; write poetry; publish collections of short-stories; write non-fiction; become a writing teacher; start a blog about writing; launch a YouTube channel on writing; do presentation coaching; create a story-telling workshop; teach kids how to write.

If you had "something with dogs," options include: dog breeder; dog trainer; dog psychologist; raising support dogs; running a dog walking service; opening a dog boarding ranch; launching an online store selling baked goods for dogs; being a portrait photographer for dogs; or, hell, going back to school and become a veterinarian.

The more variations you create from your five ideas above, the greater are the chances you'll hit on something that really sparks your imagination. Doing this drill-down for five different ideas is going to take time and mental energy, so be patient with the process — and keep activating your PEA before you start each session.

Variations on idea #1: _____

1.

2.

3.

4.

5.

Variations on idea #: 2_____

    1.

    2.

    3.

    4.

    5.

Variations on idea #3: _____

    1.

    2.

    3.

    4.

    5.

Variations on idea #4: _____

1.

2.

3.

4.

5.

Variations on idea #5: _____

1.

2.

3.

4.

5.

Way to go on digging so deep! That was a big effort. Now you have one more step in this sequence — to choose the 2-4 ideas you have the strongest connection to. The next section would be unwieldy with five or more options, so choose no more than four.

It's up to you whether you want to apply the filters of practicality or feasibility now; that could certainly help in your narrowing process. But we'll be doing that work in the final step, so if you can continue to let your thoughts run free without tying them down yet with reality, I encourage you to do so. We still have so far to go!

If you have more than four items that excite you from the drill-downs, you'll need to go back through to narrow the field. Try adding more options beyond the five variations you just did. And, while you're at it, pay attention to how your body is reacting to each of these finalists. Do they all hold the same level of excitement in your heart and in your gut, or are some stronger?

We'll be working on embodiment factors at the end of the chapter, since your ultimate choice should not come just from your analytic brain, but if it helps you to refine your choices *now* by tuning into your body, go for it.

Your 2-4 Finalists for Future Activities

1.

2.

3.

4.

4. Ignite Your Thinking

"The biggest mistake I've made
is failing to set my sights high enough."
· Grant Cardone ·

That's quite an admission by Cardone, a New York Times bestselling author in his book *The 10x Rule*. He says his failure was true in both personal and professional aspects of his life.

How about you? Do you set your sights high when considering changes in your life, or have you tended to play it safe? Or maybe you haven't really thought about it, but have just rolled along with what's in front of you, sometimes taking a big leap and other times not? I suspect this last approach is true for most people. It used to be for me.

There's great value in considering things beyond what you thought you could do. It opens you up to a greater range of possibilities and surprising twists that can turn what you want into something even more amazing. It can also significantly increase your impact.

A client of mine was captivated by the idea of opening a cidery, creating and selling artisanal ciders in a fun, funky environment. And that was enough to start him on the massive effort of learning how to make ciders and then building and launching his business. But his vision now goes far beyond that one taproom and just making cider. He still loves concocting new flavors of cider, but he really gets inspired by thinking about how to bring more fun and life to the world. So he's planning to open more taprooms, move into other delivery platforms, and get people excited about pursuing things they're passionate about. As well, he's created a new venue for live music that's really taking off and that was nowhere in his original idea of, "I'd like to open a cidery." It was by expanding his ideas of what he could do and the impact he could have that revved up his creativity.

So my promise of taking you waaaaay outside the box and waaaaay beyond what you've imagined for yourself starts now. There are two questions ahead that will challenge your thinking in ways you may never have experienced.

As you do this work, suspend your judgment. You don't need to have definitive answers for anything right now. Just stretch your thinking as far as you can. If saboteurs rise up, saying things like, "You're too old to do this!" or "Who are you to want that?" or some other kind of criticism, just reply, "Not now, friend. You can comment on this later." (And then keep deferring those voices.)

You should answer these two questions for each of the finalist ideas you've chosen. Who knows what might come up, or how one idea, stretched even further, might spark something in a different direction? Don't back off because you think it might be a lot of work. We're talking about making a big change in your life, so invest the time in yourself. Of course, if you can't get inspired to consider these questions for one of your finalists, that might indicate a limit to your enthusiasm for that option and thus you should remove it from consideration.

Question #1: What If You Couldn't Fail?

Have you ever had this thought? Most of us default to "What could go wrong?" rather than "What could go spectacularly right?" Yes, you should explore what could go wrong, but it's more useful later in the process (we'll get there in a few pages). For now, for the-sky-is-the-limit explorations, this question really sends you there.

So how would that be, to just let your mind go, and go, and go? To keep building from one idea to the next, ever heightening what's possible without fear of a dramatic failure? Not that there wouldn't be some set-backs, but that overall things just worked, and worked, and worked. If you got on that kind of train, where could you go? What more could you accomplish? And who cares about limits — let's just keep building and creating and sharing with the world.

Richard Branson comes to mind here. That man has had an extraordinary record of success. Not that everything has worked, but overall he seems to have a magic touch when it comes to building creative, compelling, high-impact businesses. And that has led to a mindset that, when he starts something new, he expects it will succeed and make a contribution to life. No wonder this guy is always smiling.

So step into a mental and emotional state where everything just *works*. Forget about "failure is not an option;" that can tighten you up. Instead, failure doesn't exist, so you are free to just get more creative and inspired the further you go.

The key to doing this exploration is to continually ask yourself, *"What else?"* Like an improv actor doing "Yes, And," just keep building and building the vision until you run out of energy. Other questions to ask yourself to push your vision higher are:

"How can this be bigger?"
"Who else can benefit from this?"
"What more could I do if money was no object?"

Here's an example. Say you want to breed dogs, specifically labradoodles. This is a significant undertaking, if you're planning on having a kennel with lots of dogs. So you could put all your energies into that and create a business, and for some people that would be enough.

But let's say you think dogs have so much to teach us and you want to spread that joy and wisdom to a larger audience than just those who buy your labradoodle pups. If you couldn't fail, what else might you do, starting from a single kennel? You could have more kennels — *and what else?* How about having a Dogs at School program, where volunteers bring dogs into elementary schools to share with the kids and teach them about the wonders of dogs? *Okay, what else?* You could create a Dog Festival in your town, to take the interactions and learning, along with games and competitions and classes, to your fellow citizens. *Great, now how can this be bigger?* We could expand these festivals all across the country. *Awesome. And who else can benefit from this?* Wow, people all over the world really. *And what if money was no object?* Fund research. Make documentaries. Create a dog sharing program. Be the #1 ambassador worldwide for dogs.

That's a very different mission than the original idea of "I'd love to breed labradoodles."

Now, nothing would require or commit you to doing all of that — or whatever you come up with in your version of this exercise. But you can see how, by imagining what else you could do, you greatly expand the range of what's possible.

A key advantage of doing this is that, with a greater vision of what you might do, it's easier to get through difficult situations because those are just steps along the way, soon to be forgotten. As well, when you've got a bigger objective in mind, even if it's a long way off, you become more aware of opportunities and things that can help you along the way. This is the case for my client with the cidery. He is attuned to things that can help his higher objective, rather than just what new flavor of cider he could create.

So for our friend, the budding breeder, he might not care about being the world's #1 dog ambassador, but by choosing a target (for now) of staging an annual Dog Festival in his community, his energies are wrapped up in something greater than just how much dog food he needs to buy this week — and his impact and enjoyment will be much higher.

In approaching this exploration, change where you will do this work. Go outside if you can; big, open skies help unleash big, open thoughts. Or go somewhere you don't usually work — maybe a new coffee shop or the quiet room at the library. Or, if home is your best option, lie on the floor and let your mind wander upwards.

As you expand your visions for what your finalist ideas could be, breathe life into them by making them as vivid and real as you can. The stronger the image and the more you can feel it in your bones, the greater is the likelihood that you can actually achieve this.

Here's a way to make sure you're really thinking big — choose things that you can't do alone, and you don't necessarily know how to do. The steps to get there aren't important right now, nor are costs or time considerations. Make the scale of these ideas as big and amazing as possible.

In fact, try using the word "amazing" as a test. As you review a given idea, ask yourself, "Is this *amazing?*" If not, keep pushing it further, or park it for a while and come back to it later.

If you struggle to use the word "amazing" to apply to something you might do, then you've definitely got limits on your thinking. *Everyone* has the potential to do amazing things in their life, so why shouldn't you?

Get out there and think BIG!

What would you do if you knew you couldn't fail?

(Answer this for each of your potential big ideas.)

Question #2: What If You Had $50 Million?

Sometimes, money can be a constraint in thoughts about the future, so let's remove that from consideration at the moment. Instead, let's swim in the river of abundance and see where that takes us. And even if you say, "But I'm not focused on money," it can be useful to envision what a lot of money could create.

So imagine that you've been given $50 million to do something amazing with each of your finalist ideas. This isn't money to fund a lavish lifestyle or buy boats or a condo in Ibiza, it's money to help you do more, much more, in the areas where you want to have an impact.

Let's say you wanted to join a mission to Nepal to improve health care services in the country. Just by going there, you will certainly help a lot of people. But imagine what else could be done if you had $50 million to bring to the efforts there. The improvements in nutrition, hygiene, sanitation, education, and services for women would be dramatically increased. You'd have money to upgrade facilities and bring in more doctors. And you would reach so many more of the poor than you could before.

That's not to say that it's all or nothing — that either you get that $50 million to share or you might as well not go. But there's something powerful in considering what a large amount of money can help you accomplish. You start to see beyond the boundaries of the job you thought you would do. It opens your eyes to the wider range of needs and opportunities. And it might even inspire you to build a foundation and raise that $50 million, because you're seeing more of the impact that such an investment can make.

Let's go back to our friend, the labradoodle breeder-to-be. What could he do with $50 million? Set up education centers in inner city locations. Fund research on the power of animals to improve our mental health. Launch Dog Festivals all over the world. Create a series on amazing dogs for Netflix.

Do you see how the possibilities for him are endless?

They can be for you, too. So, for each of your finalist ideas, think about what $50 million could help you do.

What could $50 million enable you to do?

(Answer this for each of your potential big ideas.)

5. It's Time to Choose

How did it go with the "Couldn't Fail" and "$50 Million" explorations? Is your brain weary from being stretched so far? And are all the finalist ideas still in the running or have one or more been retired?

It's now time to start comparing your finalists, on the road to choosing the one that will most inspire and sustain you. Write in your answers below for each of these questions. There's no hidden agenda to the questions nor significance to their order; they're here to help you make distinctions between your remaining candidates.

WHICH IDEA:

- has the greatest potential to inspire you for decades?

- best supports you financially?

- requires the least amount of disruption to your lifestyle?

- has the fewest hurdles or pitfalls on your journey?

- is the least expensive to achieve?

- takes the least amount of time to achieve?

- is the least complicated to put into action?

- has the greatest potential to do good for others?

Unless you've already decided on the one thing you want to pursue, your answers above probably alternated between the different ideas you've been considering. Of course, if one of your finalists was listed more often than the others, your search might be over.

Getting the most votes may not matter, however, if you're feeling some resistance to declaring a winner. The relative importance of each of the items above varies for every person, and it's possible that one of these questions might be so critical to you that its value outweighs all the other questions combined.

Below are four approaches to explore if you're still undecided.

Priorities and Points

How would you rank the questions above in terms of importance to launching and sustaining the next chapter in your life? Are some of the questions of greater significance to you than others? Take, for example, the "best supports you financially" question. For some people, this is a critical consideration and they need to give it a high priority; other people may have no financial concerns and thus don't need to rank that highly.

Once you prioritize the questions, does that shift the balance of votes toward one option? If not, you might want to go further and award points, for each question, to the various answers or choices.

One method is use a 10-point scale, with the winner of each question getting 10 points, and the other options getting a lower score. Of course, you might not want to give a full 10 points to questions with lower priorities; maybe secondary considerations max out at a 7 or a 5. Be as creative as you like with this. Once you've tallied up the scores, are you closer to a winner?

If not not, move on to the next method.

Intention and Impact

There are two key questions from earlier in this chapter that might help you decide. In fact, these questions are so important that, even if you've already got the one thing you want to do, you should check it against these two questions:

- How do you want to feel in the next chapter of your life?

- What impact do you want to have on others?

Whatever you choose to do for your next chapter, it should be in complete alignment with your answers to these two questions. If you want to feel inspired, make sure your winning idea has the potential to keep you inspired — or happy or adventurous or whatever is that key feeling you want to be wrapped in to your final days.

If the impact you want to have on people is helping them be more curious about their world — or excited, joyful, passionate, etc — your winning idea should make this easy for you to do.

Think about how each of your finalist ideas make you feel. Is there one that comes out ahead here? And think about the potential impact each one offers; how do your finalists stack up? Are your feelings and the potential impact on equal footing, or is one of those a stronger indicator of what most matters to you?

If your finalists all have relatively similar potential for you, it's time to move on to the next approach.

The 10/10/10 Test

This is a fascinating way to evaluate your choices. It's usually applied to a single decision, like "Shall I move to Maui?" Since you've got at least two finalists you're considering, you'll need to do this exercise for each one. Here's how it goes.

You will examine your feelings about each choice and the potential consequences as if it was **10 minutes** from now, **10 months** from now, and **10 years** from now. The questions you will ask for each of your finalists are, "If this is my final choice, how do I feel about that, and what are the consequences of choosing it?"

Below is an example of a form you can use; you can either create your own version or download a PDF (see the Resources section for the link). For the top line — "Decision re:" — put in what you would *do*, rather than make it a "Yes or No" type of statement. In the example, rather than write in "Should I build a retreat center?" (which implies a

Yes or No answer), put "Building a retreat center" since that's what you would do if this is your winning idea.

This concept helps you gain a wider perspective than how you're considering the choices now. And pay attention to any disconnect between how you feel at a given time and what the consequences might be. That happened to me the first time I used this. My feelings about the decision 10 minutes in the future were filled with uncertainty and doubt, but the consequences even then were clear and resolute. Plus the uncertainty and doubt were gone when I looked at the 10-month and 10-year intervals. That made my decision so much easier!

Decision re: _Building a retreat center_

	FEELINGS	CONSEQUENCES
10 MINUTES	- still conflicted - not really sure - wary of limiting myself	- can move ahead! - makes it easier to plan what to do
10 MONTHS	- occaisionally think about the other paths, but this is best	- I've gotten so much done by being all-in on this
10 YEARS	- that was one of the best decisions ever	- This place has exceeded all my expectations!

The 10/10/10 test was created by author Suzy Welch. I added my own twist by testing not just for consequences, but also feelings, since that includes in your decision the signals your body is sending out. Decisions of the caliber you are considering should not be made purely on rational or analytic factors. Your heart and your gut are sources of powerful insights.

What Does Your Body Say?

We tend to live so much of our life in our mind that we often forget that our body has a greater purpose than just propping up our head. Yes, we honor our body by feeding it and exercising it and maybe even doing meditation or other mindfulness activities. But too often, the wisdom of our body is ignored when it comes to making decisions. We default to lists of pros and cons, even while our bodies are screaming "No! No! No!" to one or more of the choices.

"Embodied self-awareness" is the key concept here, but rather than load you up with lots of research, let's do a little exercise to feel it in action.

For each of the finalists still in the running for your awesome new chapter, you're going to do a little visualization. Here are the steps:

1) Go to a quiet, comfortable place where you won't be disturbed. Close your eyes (once you've read all the instructions ;) and take several long, slow breaths.

2) Take each finalist option, one at a time, and start from the highest, most exciting image you've had of that. Think through an average day doing all the awesome things you hope to be doing. Make the visualization as rich and detailed as you can.

3) As you go through this visualization, pay close attention to how your body is reacting moment by moment. Is it calm and flowing, and maybe even a little amped up with excitement? Or are there moments where you feel some doubt or resistance to what you're experiencing? Maybe it's more subtle than that — some tension in your hands or your shoulders, or your breath is a little restricted, or your jaw is tight? Those are signs that your body is trying to be heard. As you tap into these moments, don't analyze them (yet), just notice them and then keep going with the visualization.

4) Once you finish one visualization, make some notes if you want, to help you remember the ebb and flow of your body's reactions. Then repeat the process with the other finalist(s).

5) Once you've finished all the visualizations, sit for a few minutes and tune into what your body wants to tell you about the exercise. Don't force an answer on yourself, just be open to whatever wants to come into your consciousness.

What did you notice? Is anything clearer to you about one or more of the finalists, either that you are even more excited about it or that you hadn't realized you've been resisting it in some way? Whatever you've been feeling is information, so pay attention to it.

Of course, it's a long way from "I feel a little pressure in my head" to "This is never going to work! What was I thinking?" But they *are* connected. It's not that your success or failure is contingent on what's happening in your body, but what's happening in your body *does* contribute to your success or failure. The more you pay attention to how you're *being*, not just in your thinking but in your body, the greater is your clarity and your ability to make the wisest choice.

Are you there now? If you have a winner, write it in the box below. And congratulations! But if you're still wavering (hopefully on only two choices now), let's go to a final consideration.

If You're Still Not Sure . . .

In the business world, there's a popular concept called "lean startups." These are companies just getting started, which create a "minimum viable product" (MVP) and then see if anyone is interested in it. Since success can be fickle, they want to find out as quickly and cheaply as possible whether a concept generates interest or is destined to fail. In fact, "fail fast" is revered in the startup world.

You can borrow the same concept to test out your last surviving ideas. Basically, you find ways to try out each path in smaller versions or iterations, focusing on learning, and not worrying about the results.

If you want to start a bakery, create a small product line and test it at a nearby farmer's market. If you're interested in being part of an aid mission overseas, get involved with a nearby program first. If you want to breed dogs, find a local breeder who will let you help out for a couple weeks, just to get a sense of what the job really entails.

There are lots of ways to create little tests, so get yourself into apprentice mode and see how you really feel about these options you're considering.

And the winner is:

Launching Your Next Chapter

If everything seems under control,
you're not going fast enough.
· Mario Andretti ·

You probably didn't expect this quote from famed race driver Mario Andretti, did you? After all, you've been deep into discovering what will make for a fabulous new direction for your life, and taking your time with it, as I've urged. Maybe you thought I would start with something gentle, like Lao Tzu's classic line, "A journey of a thousand miles begins with a single step."

I included Andretti's quote, not because you should go faster — speed isn't important here — but because *not* having everything under control matters a lot.

We touched on this in the *What Could Hold You Back?* section of the *Taking Stock* chapter and it bears repeating. If you need to see every step of your journey before you begin, if you need to have everything plotted out and under control, you either A) won't get started, B) will limit where and how far you go, or C) may grind to a halt if something doesn't go according to plan.

The thing is, you won't know all the steps in advance. And that should be okay. If you are committed to the journey, you will have the flexibility and resilience to keep going. And, if you trust the process — and your creativity — the right steps will appear when you need them.

This reminds me of when I wrote two novels, back in the 1990s. Some people plot their books down to the finest detail, knowing in advance everything that happens when, where, and to whom, almost down to the amount of ice left in their drinks when they leave the bar. Their story is virtually done before they type a single word.

My process was nothing like that. With both books, I knew who the main characters were and the motivations that drove each of them, I knew how I wanted to start each book, and I knew what the climax should be; I was writing high-tech thrillers, so there had to be a dramatic climax.

For most of each book, though, I had no idea when I began writing what would happen. I had some vague ideas, kind of like milestones that I had to reach, but otherwise it was unformed. That left me free, as I sat down at my computer each day, to discover what was going to happen alongside my readers. It enabled a freshness that might not have been there if I had meticulously plotted every last moment in advance. When it felt like someone new needed to enter the story, they appeared in my head with very little effort. I can think of four pivotal characters in each book who were surprises for me, as well as plot twists that seemed to come out of the blue at just the moment the story needed them.

Writing was, for me, a constant act of discovery. And in those moments of discovery I felt most alive. (And still do.) I hope your reinvention will be the same!

Here's where we're going in this chapter:

1. Define Your Roadmap

2. Declare Your Commitments

3. Plan the Next 90 Days

4. Focus on Small Steps

5. Set Up a Routine

6. Don't Go It Alone

7. Be Patient

1. Define Your Roadmap

So, what do you need to do first? Map out your journey! Defining the major milestones or achievements in your journey, with a clear vision of where you're headed, provides a structure to guide your decisions on both macro and micro levels. How you actually get to your destination, or even to each milestone, may change from moment to moment, but as long as you can see where you're headed — and you believe in your journey — you'll be able to handle any rough roads.

In defining the map of your journey, you don't have to actually draw it out with pen and paper. You can write a rough outline on paper, in a computer file, or in this book.

The switch I'd like you to make, in deciding on your major milestones, is to work *backwards* from your objective.

If you start from today and work forward, it's easy to get buried in details. You might get so hooked by questions and dependencies and things you need and . . . It's exhausting just to think about it.

This creates a mindset of *lack*, of things you haven't done and obstacles in your way. When you're locked into lack, the work can easily become a grind and you could quickly get derailed. You might have days where you say "F.U." to lack and you get shit done. But when all you can see is what's in front of your nose, it increases the chances that you'll get bogged down and maybe even decide to quit.

What you want instead is a sense of *fait accompli* — the idea that this has already happened. That thought blows away the concept of lack, because, hey, you've already made it! If you start from your destination and work backwards, you don't need evidence that you're making progress; progress has already been achieved. This relieves stress and doubt, which allows you to think more freely, and that is what will help you the most.

Neuroscience endorses this approach of working backwards from your goal. In the book, *Helping People Change* by Richard Boyatzis, Melvin Smith, and Ellen Van Oosten, the authors make the case that "change cannot be focused on primarily fixing problems, but instead must connect to that person's positive vision of themselves or to an inspiring vision or goal they've long held." Through extensive research, they have shown that we're far more creative and effective when we start from our dreams and work backwards, rather than pushing forward to solve one problem, and then the next and the next.

So how do you do this? Let's take our example of breeding dogs.

Suppose you want to be a breeder who energizes your community around these wonderful animals and creates a happy, supportive world for both humans and dogs.

You *could* get overwhelmed by details at the beginning, like where to locate the kennel, how you're going to pay for it, what the tax implications are going to be — and get so swamped that you might never see the joyous light of dog nirvana that originally captured your imagination.

OR . . . you could start with thinking about staging a dog festival in autumn that will really bring your new community together, and then work backwards from there. If I gave you the challenge of having only four milestones between that amazing event and today, what might they be?

GOAL: Autumn Dog Festival!

Milestone #4: Teach dogs amazing tricks.

Milestone #3: Develop a borrow-a-dog program in the community.

Milestone #2: Create Dogs at School program

Milestone #1: Establish kennel.

Today: Nothing but a dream.

If you just started from today, working towards Milestone #1 with little thought of what might follow that beyond a vague "festival" idea, there are dozens of things that could distract or derail you. And if all you see is the day-to-day drudge of just getting the place running, you might never reach your dream of having an Autumn Dog Festival.

BUT . . . If you start by defining the major milestones above, your mind is going to be working on Milestones 2, 3, and 4 even when you're setting up the dog pens. It makes menial tasks easier to deal with when you've got the alluring vision of dogs at school and in people's homes and, finally, as the star attraction at the festival.

There's a wonderful example of this in the book *The Power of Meaning* by Emily Esfahani Smith. She describes a zookeeper, Ashley, who spends 80% of her time doing routine tasks, including shoveling giraffe poop, and only 20% of her time doing fun or intellectually challenging work like training the animals. Yet Ashley *loves* her job. Smith writes: "Even menial tasks are meaningful for Ashely because they're tied to her broader purpose of keeping the animals healthy and engaged." With her goal fixed in her mind and in her heart, she can handle all kinds of shit — literally.

Starting at the end and working backwards doesn't mean you'll magically have all the steps laid out for you; remember, you're not going to see every step in the journey before you start. But with enough structure to guide your actions over the days, weeks, and months ahead, you can bring your full self and all your creativity to the moment without worrying about "Is this the right step?"

By the way, it's not just about reaching your goal. As Ralph Waldo Emerson said: "Life is a journey, not a destination."

What's your big dream?

What's Milestone #4?

What's Milestone #3?

What's Milestone #2?

What's Milestone #1?

2. Declare Your Commitments

Before jumping into action, let's nail down some things that will help keep you on course. I'm talking commitments. Commitments to the things you will do and won't do, as well as commitments for how you're going to be and not be while doing all you're doing. We're taking a wholistic approach, not just "And then I do this. And then I do that. And then..."

Why a wholistic approach? Because it will help keep you focused. Life is full of "shiny objects" — of things you could do or have, of things you might try or things that can distract you from doing the hard work that reinvention requires. Friends, family, and the internet are only too quick and too happy to offer you alternatives to what you might otherwise be doing. It's almost like they're waiting to sabotage your commitments and new objectives.

Shiny objects or distractions are like being on a diet and having a rich, tantalizing cake set right in front of you. Do you 1) lunge for the cake, 2) take a little of the frosting, which keeps that lure working on your mind, or 3) walk past it without even a pause?

We're aiming for a walk-past-without-a-pause mindset. And, being human, that won't always be easy. In fact, sometimes you might even lunge for the whole cake. That's okay; it's important to acknowledge your humanity. What you want to avoid is getting so diverted that you cripple your progress toward your fabulous future.

To help you stay on course and be able to recover quickly when you're diverted, here's something I call a Commitment Matrix. On a piece of paper, draw a chart like you see below. (See the Resources section for a link to a PDF form.) Fill this out for your first milestone, then repeat this exercise when you are ready for the next milestone. You'll find instructions and a completed sample below.

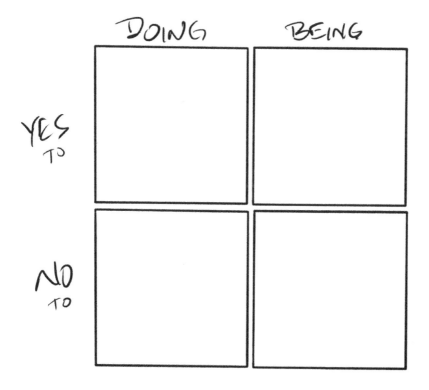

Here's how to fill out each box:

· The **Yes to Doing** box is exactly what you'd expect — the things you will commit to doing to get to your first milestone. Don't try to cram in every To Do item; just pick your three or four most important actions for this milestone.

· The **Yes to Being** box captures the types of emotions you want to experience during this milestone. Think positive emotions, like happy, adaptable, and inspired, or animating ones like focused, resourceful, and committed.

· The **No to Doing** box is where you list things you will *not* do on your way to the first milestone, like taking three months off. These declarations keep you on track when shiny objects or a desire to take an easier path appears. Just know that you need to start saying "No" to things.

· The **No to Being** box may feel the most unfamiliar at first. This is where you say "Hell, No!" to fears and saboteurs with words like hesitant, scared, and wimpy.

Take your time with this exercise. The goal is to write three or four items in each box. You can go in any order, jump around as things occur to you, and you might even do several iterations until you get it just right.

Let's use the breeding dogs idea as an example of how you'd fill this out. You will play the part of the breeder-to-be.

So you've settled on breeding labradoodles and you suddenly think "What do I do now? Do I buy an existing kennel? Buy land and build it? Arrange for a shipment of breeding dogs, just so I won't procrastinate on finding them a new home? Or should I incorporate 'Big Dog, Inc.' to put the stamp of reality on this venture from the start?"

And then there are all the people to inform of your decision, and you'll have to put your current house on the market, and your nephew Danny really wants to name all the dogs and he wants to do it *now*.

Ooof. Life is getting complicated already!

So you decide to fill in a Commitment Matrix to help refine your plan of attack. After a lot of thinking, here's what you've come up with (in bullet-point format):

I'm saying YES to DOING

· Developing a cost/benefit analysis on buying v. building a kennel.
· Finding a community where my family will be happy to live.
· Finding a source for 10 happily-raised labradoodles.
· Incorporating "Big Dog, Inc."

I'm saying YES to BEING

· Happy about my choice of breeding dogs, even on rough days.
· Enthusiastic in sharing my dream with others.
· Confident that I made the right decision, regardless of the cost.
· Grateful for the opportunity to bring doodle-love to the world.

I'm saying NO to DOING

· Trying to scale up too fast.
· Working 24/7.
· Letting my wife talk me out of this.
· Letting the dogs sleep in our bed.

I'm saying NO to BEING

· Hesitant.
· Overwhelmed.
· Arrogant about my vision.
· Freaked out by any cost overruns.

Do you get the power and richness of this approach? Suddenly, it's not just a bunch of steps you have to do; you now have both clarity and conviction that will keep you going no matter what happens. No Gantt chart on earth has that kind of mobilizing effect. Yes, you'll still have lots of things to do, but your sense of purpose is ignited!

Giving credit where credit is due, I learned this exercise during my coach training with CTI (Co-Active Training Institute). This stuff works.

Here's how the form might look for our labradoodle-loving friend.

3. Plan the Next 90 Days

So you're psyched about your milestones and your commitments are clear. That's great. But I'm not going to send you off now with a hearty pat on the back and bright wishes of "I hope you figure out how to get there…" Nope, I'm in this with you for the long haul, so we're going to do some planning.

There's a gap between today and that first milestone. And while you can figure out what to do *today*, let's put a framework in place for how to get to that first milestone and beyond.

Here's an example. Let's say you want to drive from L.A. to New York City, and your first milestone is to see the Grand Canyon, a distance of 500 miles. Is that enough to send you on your way — like just jump in the car and follow the signs or listen to your GPS? Hell, no. Do you really want to go through Barstow, Needles, and Kingman (Zzzzz), or would you rather take a little longer trip and go through Sedona, by way of Phoenix? (Yes, please!)

It's the same with your quest. You have to make some choices and you need a goal for one or more points in between today and your first milestone. This is like setting secondary milestones between your major ones. But we're going to add a twist to keep you moving forward.

Here's how to do this: build your plans around what you want to achieve *in the next 90 days*. That timing is enough to give you flexibility in how you approach the work, without making it either too big a period, which a year might be, or too short or restrictive, which a month might be. 90 days gives you a chance to try things out without fearing that you don't have time to start again. But it also isn't such a generous amount of time that you can piddle around for five months and then try to cram all the work into one month.

It's the combination of timing and what you want to get done in 90 days that makes the difference. If you really want to get moving on this, set ambitious targets for what you want to achieve. On the other hand, if you plan to take some time to travel or you've got a weekly date with your grandkids, you might set less demanding targets.

Let's look at our friend the dog breeder to see how he might design his first 90 days. If he's really driven, he might plan to get his business licensed, line up bank financing, borrow every book from the library about raising dogs, buy a property, build the dog runs, and locate the dogs to breed. If, however, his wife reminds him of the trip to Bali that he'd long promised they'd take, he might only get three items on the list done in 90 days.

There are no medals given out for who gets the most stuff done. Rather, there's the peace-of-mind medal you achieve when you know you're moving forward at whatever pace fits your needs right now. And having a fence around those 90 days helps you be realistic about what you can and can't accomplish. The key is to ask yourself, "What can I get done in the next 90 days?" Once you reach the end of that period, set your goals for the next 90 days. Then repeat as needed.

What are your goals for the next 90 days?

4. Focus on Small Steps

Here's one last reminder before you leap into action: It's not a race; you will get there eventually. In the meantime, you will be best served by focusing on what is right in front of your toes.

Big, sustainable change happens in small shifts, not through massive blow-up-your-life kinds of efforts. This isn't a spin on Aesop's fable of *The Tortoise and the Hare*, because even the most impetuous of us aren't arrogantly messing around when we get a big lead; we just get too far ahead of ourselves sometimes and leave out important steps. I've done that before.

So what does it take to be consistently and sustainably moving toward your goal? To keep from burning out? And to ensure you don't skip over something important to your growth?

It takes small steps.

And more small steps.

And mix in some variety.

And take breaks periodically.

And then go back to small steps.

(Repeat as needed)

Big leaps are fun. Big leaps are energizing. And the riff above about small steps doesn't mean you can't also make some big leaps. But don't rely on big leaps to get you to your goal. Doing so could make your efforts a non-starter if the leap seems overwhelming or you can't imagine what the next big leap should be. Instead, it's the consistency and discipline of those small steps that will break down bigger objectives and ultimately get you to where you're going.

Speaking of big leaps, sometimes things *do* happen in a flash, where you suddenly achieve something big or get absolute clarity about what comes next and how you'll be. Those are moments to cherish. But there's no guarantee you can invoke them on command. They typically appear after taking a lot of small steps first and sometimes going sideways or backwards in order to go forward.

It's like slogging through a jungle with lots of thick brush in your way, forcing you to just grind out step after step. And sometimes you need to go around a massive tree that's blocking your path. Then, suddenly, you break free into open ground and can surge ahead.

Understanding and accepting this slow/fast dynamic will make the whole effort more tolerable. And when things bog down — and they will, which is why there's a whole chapter coming up on getting through the muck — you'll be glad to have the mantra of small steps to fall back on. If you're ever left thinking, "What do I do now?", just ask yourself what's the next smallest step you can take.

Consistency is everything.

What's the smallest step you can take right now?

(Repeat, repeat, repeat)

5. Set Up a Routine

The next part is to create a plan for how you're going to approach your work every day. EVERY DAY. This includes where and when you'll work on this. Specificity does wonders here.

When you wake up knowing how your day is structured, it makes it significantly easier to *do* the work. This is much more productive and effective than thinking "What shall I do today?" or "I ought to do some stuff on the Me 2.0 plan."

That doesn't mean you have to devote hours each day to working on this; a five-minute progress check might be enough for the weekend. But nail down your overall attack plan with your days, weeks, and months in mind. If your milestones and your 90-day plans are the "What" you're doing, your routine covers the "When" and "How" of your process.

This might seem like overkill, and if anyone is wired to resist such structure, it's me. But this book is a perfect example of the power of intentional design. I decided in April 2019 to write this book. It would have been very easy to just think about that idea and tell people that I was going to write this book, and still be spouting that tale months and years later. That's the case, in fact, with my third novel, "Big Weed." It's a great title and the concept just delights and inspires me, and yet I haven't gotten myself to write it more than five years after I got the idea. I won't bore you with the details, but I own that reality.

This book, however, is different. Similar to when the idea for my first novel slammed into my head and wouldn't leave, the idea for *F*ck*

170

Retirement grabbed me and wouldn't let go. It compelled me to write it. I knew, though, that if I was really going to do this, I had to make a commitment to consistent effort, so . . .

I committed to writing two hours a day, every day, for the month of May 2019, just to get it off the ground. As I write this, I'm on Day 28 and I haven't missed a day yet. I'm at about 25,000 words, so maybe half way? (I'm jumping around with these chapters.)

I couldn't stop my other work and just focus on the book, though, so this commitment also required me to get to bed earlier, which is tough for a lifelong night owl, and then get working earlier. 28 days in, and my body now wakes me before 6 AM every day.

But I didn't just snap my fingers and was instantly on a new schedule, tapping merrily at my keyboard every morning. It has been a grind on many of those 28 days just to get myself to write. Earlier in the month, I was having sleep problems and would sit down at my computer with only a couple hours of rest in me. Or the mornings where I just didn't know what I was going to write about. Or when I had coaching clients early in the day, so I couldn't get to writing until the afternoon. Some days, I just didn't feel it.

AND YET . . . I showed up. Every damned day. I sat down and nudged myself until a trickle of inspiration seeped in, and then I was off to the races. I have not had one day yet where, at the end of the session, I didn't feel good about what I wrote. Sure, some things had to be tweaked the next day, but that's part of the writing process. And I finally have a rhythm to this effort; my body just moves towards my desk at 7 AM, and that feels nice.

Speaking of showing up and being open to what may come, this section is a perfect example. I was going to write about something else today. This section didn't even exist in my head until two hours ago when I thought, "Oh, I should write about having a routine."

As you are reinventing yourself, be open to these gifts of insight or direction that are offered to you. And make no mistake, they are out there for you. They may not have ribbons around them and little sparkly lights that say, "Open me!" But the insights and inspirations that can propel you forward are absolutely there, whispering in your ear. You just need to pay attention.

If you're still employed, create a schedule for the open times in your day when you'll do *something* on this process of reinventing yourself, even if it's just for five minutes. If you're not employed, or underemployed, it's critical that you set a daily structure now. Then just keep showing up and you'll be unstoppable.

Six Months Later . . .

It is now November 2019. What an interesting adventure since I wrote the words above. I crossed the finish line on May 31st, having written every day that month. By then, I needed to crawl out of my cave and talk to people about their experiences relative to retirement, as evidenced in the 2nd chapter and in many of the stories throughout this book.

But I lost my iron-clad routine. I was still working on things for the book, but I wrote very little and allowed *many* things to steal my focus. I was aware of my growing distance from this project, but I couldn't turn it around right away.

Once my month of deep research was done, I went further adrift, pulled by other projects that demanded my attention. Ugh. Finally, in August, I decided to again try the write-every-day-of-the-month routine, but that lasted only three days. (Did you notice the clue in that last sentence? I decided to "try," which is infinitely less committed than "I am going to.")

In mid-September, I realized that there were too many distractions in my home office — too many things that could delay my daily start and keep me from getting as deep as I needed to. Some people can work amidst chaos, and even thrive within it, but I need a cone of silence and a distraction-free zone to do my best work. This is why I, and many others, find plane flights to be wonderfully productive places.

So without waiting for a new month to roll around, I started going to a nearby Panera Bread store, with just a laptop, noise-cancelling headphones, and my conviction. I'm there a little after 6 AM on weekdays and 7 AM on weekends, and I go every day. I'm such a regular that one guy behind the counter puts together my usual order as soon as he sees me walk through the door. (Cinnamon Raisin bagel and a hot tea. Thanks, Bubba!)

The thing is, I found my routine again, and without the artificial structure of writing every day in a given month. I'm just going every day, without fail. This is my new reality until I finish the book. I've gone from "I hope I can do this" to "I am going to fucking do this no matter what." That last sentence didn't even need an exclamation point on it. I don't have to pump myself up to do this, it is just flat out happening. That's the kind of conviction you'll want, where it's so deep and final that nothing will deter you.

To be clear, I don't spend all day at Panera. I put in a solid two to three hours, then head home, where I take care of other business or do further work on the book. It's a fantastic feeling to walk into the house at 9 AM, with several hours of focused writing already accomplished. My wife is so inspired by my routine that she joins me at Panera every morning.

Now, I wouldn't ask you to repeat my routine exactly. You might not be a "morning person," which I was definitely not six months ago, and you might not be as obsessive as I can get when I'm consumed by a project. But find a routine that lets you get deeply into this work *and* that you can sustain. If you can approach this with excitement and anticipation, and be dedicated to the work on a regular basis, you will make incredible progress.

Do Something Every Day

To really set yourself up for success, make sure you do something every day, even if it's just five minutes. Small steps, done daily, take you far.

Here's a great example. Matthew Dicks was an elementary school teacher and aspiring writer, who got hooked on the stories he heard on *The Moth Radio Hour* on NPR. (The Moth is an international storytelling organization and their work is fantastic!) At first, storytelling seemed to him to be "mysterious and impossible," as he recounts in his book *Storyworthy*. But once he got a taste of standing in front of an audience telling stories, he was hooked.

To help himself learn, and build a catalog of stories, he dedicated himself to writing something, anything, every day. Even if he only spent five minutes making notes on something that had happened that morning, he put fingers to keyboard every day. Here's how he describes his process, which he calls "Homework for Life."

"By creating a system requiring that I only write a few sentences a day, I was also sure that I'd never miss a day, and this is important. Miss one day, and you'll allow yourself to miss two. Miss two days, and you'll skip a week. Skip a week and you're no longer doing your Homework for Life."

This dedication, and a passion for storytelling, led to him become a top storyteller, winning 45 Moth StorySLAM competitions and being crowned GrandSLAM champion six times. He has written a book about how to become an accomplished storyteller, the aforementioned, and wonderful, *Storyworthy*.

That kind of daily practice, that commitment to consistency, creates momentum. You can take it further by adding a daily check-in with yourself on how you're doing. Ask yourself questions like "What went well today? What didn't go well? What did I learn and how will I be smarter tomorrow?" Being consistent about this allows you to be clear on where you are in your journey and how you might need to adjust, when adjusting is easier and more incremental. The best way to do this is to write the questions and your answers in a journal. That gives you a through-line you can return to when things start to get sideways. (Hat tip to Tasha Eurich's book *Insight* for this idea.)

Get Locked In Right Away

We've been talking about having a plan for each day, but how do you actually get started? If you just sit down at your desk, it can be too easy to get sidetracked by little diversions or get hooked by your NEA (negative emotional attractors). What will help is to have a start-up routine, kind of like turning on a sign that says, "Open for Business." To get locked into the day's work and clear out any crap that might be lingering in your mind, here are some ideas for how to begin your day.

- Make a playlist of songs that get you pumped up and ready to conquer the world. Play it as you get yourself ready to go.

▪ Create a little dance routine, do a yoga sequence, jog around the house, shadow box, or choose some other physical activity that gets your *body* into the game, not just your head.

▪ Do a short meditation to calm you down and clear away whatever had been swirling in your mind.

There are countless other things you might do or devices you might employ — vision boards, anyone? — to get you totally present in *Now*. Find something that makes it easy for you to get centered and focused and ready to give your full effort to this very important work.

How will you structure your day?

What small thing can you do every day to keep yourself going?

How will you kick off each day's work?

Celebrate Regularly

The last part of setting a routine is to make sure you celebrate your progress. If your journey becomes one long grind, where you're toiling away with no end in sight, it's easy to lose momentum and passion for this work. So stop periodically and celebrate your achievements! You're doing amazing work; you deserve to be honored for it, even if you have to do the honoring yourself. Celebrations can be as simple or as elaborate you please.

The point is to do this regularly, and to delight in it! My wife and I have this silly little dance we do together whenever one of us achieves something new. It's dumb, but it's so fun and it makes us realize that we're not just slogging along. Many sales groups ring a bell when they close a big deal, as a way of saying "Way to go!" to the team. The possibilities are endless.

How will you celebrate your progress, in small ways and large?

6. Don't Go It Alone

It's hard to do it all alone. I know; I've been there too often. There are some positives to the solo path, but they are outweighed by what others can bring to your quest and how they can support you. Among the advantages:

1) They've had experiences you haven't had, which can provide critical and perhaps unexpected insights to help your efforts. As accomplished as you are, there is a whole universe of things you haven't done, places you haven't gone, ideas you haven't explored. Involving others helps multiply your efforts.

2) They can see your blind spots, which is particularly important in doing the work of reinvention. They can help you sidestep potential disasters, particularly ones you might have a habit of repeating, and invite you to explore new ways of doing things that can speed up your journey to a reinvented you.

3) They can champion you, cheering you on when you're doubting yourself or feeling weary in the quest. Just knowing you're not alone and that someone is rooting for you to succeed is very important to maintaining momentum. Their support amplifies all your efforts to expand and grow.

4) They bring their sphere of influence into the environment, opening doors you might not be able to open yourself.

How do you enlist others in your journey, as partners walking by your side? How can they share your load and divide your tasks? You and they get to decide what that looks like, but start thinking now about your journey as a group endeavor.

Getting others involved does require you to be selective, however. If some people in your life want you to stay on a safe, familiar path, they're not likely to enhance or inspire your efforts. Whether that's a family member or someone with a vested interest in the status quo — which means you *not* changing — you won't want to share every detail of what you're doing. If you have people who expect you to make predictable choices, it's time to go elsewhere for help.

Look for a friend, trusted colleague, or someone who could be an advisor, mentor, or sounding board. Figure out first what kind of help you need, then try to find the best fit for that role. What is critically important is that they be non-judgmental. Where you're going has to come from *your* vision, not their idea of where you ought go.

You should, of course, consider hiring a coach. One advantage of having a coach is that they have no expectations for what you're trying to do or how you want to get there. They are trained to work with you from where you are right now and will be focused on helping you reach the fullest expression of you, whatever that may be. They will help you uncover your blind spots, will champion you when things get tough, will challenge you when they think you're avoiding the truth, and will sit and listen when you just need *someone* to hear you out.

In considering a coach, don't get hung up on labels, such as "life coach" or "executive coach" or "transformational coach." While many people have a particular focus for their practice and there are lots of schools that certify coaches, ultimately we coaches all do the same things — we get in touch with where you are now and where you want to be, listen hard, ask powerful questions, and help you see yourself and your future in new ways.

Find *someone* who can help you navigate the path to a bright new version of You. And remember that you are always in charge. Involving others does not have to dilute or divert your plans. The right partner can make a world of difference.

What kind of help do you need, or could you use?

Who can you get to help you in your journey?

Find An Accountability Buddy

Another flavor of not going it alone is to have an accountability buddy. This is not as involved as having a partner in your reinvention efforts, but is no less important. Having someone who holds you accountable for doing this work increases the likelihood that you'll actually achieve your goals. What that accountability looks like — how you report in, how involved they are in your process, what consequences they impose if you don't meet your objectives — is up to you.

I had an accountability buddy (or "AB") for the first phase of creating this book, my write-for-two-hours-every-day-in-May routine. I committed to texting her every day once I finished my writing. There were no penalties established, and I'm sure she would've been cool if I had missed a day, but committing to checking in with her daily was one more thing to help ensure that I actually did the writing.

Here's another AB story. For 14 years, I had wanted to run a marathon. When I finally stood at the starting line for my first marathon, my friend, Joe, was waiting for me at Mile 22. I ran fast — too fast — for 18 miles, and then hit the proverbial wall. It was awful! I started walking a little bit, then running again, walking a little longer, then running, and so on. The one thing that kept me from giving in to my misery and quitting was knowing that Joe was waiting for me at Mile 22. And, Joe being Joe, there would've been hell to pay if I didn't show up at Mile 22.

So I gutted it out for the next four miles, until I finally saw Joe leaping up and down shouting, "Windsor! Windsor! Windsor!" I was suffering so much I could barely acknowledge his joyful presence, and I couldn't pick up my pace despite his urging. Knowing he was there, however, absolutely got me as far as Mile 22. After that, I had only 4.2 more miles to go, so I plodded along to the finish line. Having an AB saved my dream!

Who will be your accountability buddy?

How will you be accountable to her/him?

7. Be Patient

You're on a long road, no matter where you're going in your reinvention. But it doesn't have to feel like that, if your focus is on the journey itself and not just the destination. Being in the present moment makes it easier to weather storms.

It also helps when you don't flirt with burnout by trying to do this in one big push. You need to take breaks from time-to-time. In fact, deliberate rest is critical to doing your best, most creative work. Rest should not be something that happens if you somehow manage to fit it into your busy day; rest is something that elevates everything you do. Alex Soojung-Kim Pang, in his book *Rest: Why You Get More Done When You Work Less* argues that you should make rest a priority, even to the point of putting it into your calendar.

In his extensively researched book, Pang builds a strong case for not working to exhaustion. In fact, he cites multiple studies that indicate four hours a day is the optimal amount of time you should devote to focused work. FOUR HOURS. From Dickens to Darwin to Ingmar Bergman, great minds in all fields seem to have optimized their days around a four-hour focus on work.

Included in the book is a fascinating study done in the 1950s about the productivity of the science faculty at the Illinois Institute of Technology. Researchers Raymond Van Zelst and Willard Kerr studied their colleagues' work habits and schedules, then graphed these data against the number of articles they produced. Alex Pang says you might expect the result would be a straight line showing that the more hours the scientists worked, the more articles they would publish. But the graph turned out very differently.

What the researchers found was an M-shaped plot. Here are some of the key findings:

- The productivity peaks were between 10-20 hours per week and 40-45 hours per week.

- Scientists who spent 25 hours in the workplace were no more productive than those who spent five hours at work. (What?!) People who put in 50 hours per week were also about as productive as those who spent five hours. The researchers speculated that this 50-hour group probably required continuous use of bulky equipment.

- The least productive of all were those who put in 60-hour weeks.

So ease up on the reins. You don't have to run yourself into the ground to make your quest happen. Focus on small steps, work every day, give yourself breaks — and then go all out when you're really onto something exciting and want to work on it every waking hour. These ebbs and flows in how you apply your energy will help you do your best work over the long run. If your vision is strong and your dedication is locked in, you'll eventually achieve your goal.

Take a Time-Out

Some days, despite all your best intentions, you will get bogged down. Some days, it won't feel like you're on the downslope of a roller coaster, it will feel like everything is going straight to hell.

It's easy, when you're in the muck, to lose your sense of who you are or what you really want. You may begin to doubt yourself with thoughts like:

"Am I really up for this?"
"There must be an easier way."
"I'm not sure I want it *that* much."
And the perennial "I'm too old for this."

Okay, take a deep breath and let it out slowly. Do that again.

Struggling, and even suffering, are normal parts of such a significant change effort. This is not a time to beat yourself up because you can't maintain a high pace or feel like you're not making headway. This is a time to acknowledge that the most rewarding climbs have bumpy paths that go up *and* down. So pause a moment and look back at how far you've come already.

This is a time for self-compassion. You're doing important work, for yourself and for the world. Every now and then, you need to ease up on the pressure and allow yourself to be human, to have highs and lows, and even the occasional stumble. Take time to recharge, get out in nature if you can, and be sure to celebrate your progress.

But if it feels like a time-out isn't enough, don't despair. The next chapter will help you embrace the struggle and be stronger because of all you've gone through. This is a marathon effort and you're only at mile 18.

Embracing the Struggle

If I didn't start walking the path of most resistance,
I would end up in this mental hell forever.
· David Goggins ·

What a concept, huh? The path of *most* resistance, the path of *maximum discomfort.* Could you do that? What would it even look like? Forcing yourself to reach out to strangers? Continuing to pursue your plan when it seems like you're not making progress? Dealing with so much "well-meaning" advice that you should stop what you're doing? Ugh. Being a trailblazer in your own life can be *rough.* And chances are high that you will face these kinds of moments.

When you don't give in, when you push through the resistance, when you've done that hard thing and still find yourself breathing, you'll have opened up new opportunities, strengthened your resilience, and proven to yourself that you're capable of more than you imagined. *(You've probably also lengthened your telomeres and increased your longevity!)* It's exciting, liberating territory — until the next big challenge or wall of resistance appears, and then you have to repeat the I-can-do-this routine all over again.

The thing is, it doesn't have to feel horrible and stifling; it doesn't have to look like you only have suffering ahead and you'll never get to your goal. Progress happens in small steps and consistent effort — and enjoying the fucking ride. Your mindset on all this is critical. Will you approach the challenging parts as something you have to submit to, or as something to be conquered?

One of the masters of mindset is the author of the quote above, David Goggins. A retired Navy Seal and one of the world's most badass ultra-endurance athletes, his book, *Can't Hurt Me: Master Your Mind and Defy the Odds*, is filled stories of epic challenges and heroic efforts to survive and thrive. Perhaps his biggest success was transforming himself from a depressed, obese young man who had repeatedly given up on himself to someone who has endured some of the most physically demanding competitions and trials on the planet.

The lessons Goggins provides go way beyond just extreme physical pursuits; they apply to accomplishing anything in life that really matters to you. His message is less about what you're *doing* and more about how you're thinking and *being* in the face of struggles.

While some of his exploits may seem crazy, like doing a 100-mile race on three days notice, he provides incredible examples of what extreme dedication can achieve. At one point, astonished after gutting out a very fast marathon time when he hadn't been able to run even a mile the day before, he asked himself: *"What am I capable of?"*

That's the question you need to ask yourself, particularly if you are feeling stuck, stuck, stuck, stuck, stuck. That's what you need to ask when you feel like things are not working and you want to give up. As Goggins illustrates, there are few limits to what you can do.

What would you be capable of doing if you didn't feel stuck?

What could make that happen?

Another book that can help here is *The Obstacle Is The Way: The Timeless Art of Turning Trials Into Triumphs* by Ryan Hoover. Based on the writings of Roman general Marcus Aurelius and the philosophies of the Stoics, this book argues that obstacles don't inhibit success, they *create* it. Or, as Hoover writes, "What stands in the way becomes the way."

So, instead of looking at impediments as something bad, try seeing them as gifts to help get you to your objective faster. That might seem absurd, if you're frustrated or fearful about where things are going — particularly if you're not seeing daylight ahead of you on the path to the shining vision of your new chapter.

But if you *allow* the possibility that what you most need to help you is wrapped up in what's holding you back, you create the space for magic to happen. Unlike in fairy tales, however, the magic doesn't appear in a swirl of sparkles, it shows up quietly when you step into your discomfort and do the hard things you need to do to move ahead.

Those hard things could be conversations you need to have. They could be in saying "No" when others expect you to say "Yes." They could be risks you need to take. They might be in throwing out the last three months of work to take a new path toward your ultimate goal. Or they might be ignoring all the chatter about how you're not making progress and you should really rethink this and maybe you should see if Walmart is hiring greeters.

The chatter, by the way, is likely to be loudest and most persistent in your own head, but you don't have to believe that BS. You're also likely to hear it from others, particularly well-meaning partners. You must ignore all that well-intentioned advice, both external and internal.

Reinventing yourself requires that you not let *anything* stop you from achieving what you want. Sometimes that means going through an obstacle, sometimes it requires going around it or finding a different path, sometimes it requires patience to outlast whatever is holding you back, and sometimes it means going back to the proverbial drawing board. It is not a sign of failure if you decide to restart the process; instead, it is a sign of wisdom.

Among the things that will help you are to be objective about what you're facing, keep the negative voices in your head quiet, and focus only on what you can control.

Let that sink in for a moment — *Focus only on what you can control.* Anything else is a waste of time, energy, and hope.

Right now, what obstacles do you face?

Right now, what things can you control?

A third book with useful perspectives is Seth Godin's *The Dip: A Little Book That Teaches You When to Quit (and When to Stick)*. What we want to look at is the dip; the sticking part comes later.

The dip is that part of your journey where things get difficult, where it seems like you're just going down at a time when you want to continue going up. It's during the dip that most people and companies give up their big effort to produce something fabulous, just when they should be forging ahead.

But it's hard to keep going when you're in the middle of the dip, because you can't easily see when, or if, it will end. As Godin mentions, nobody quits a marathon in the 25th mile because they realize the finish is so close (I can attest to that!), but when you're in the dip, you don't see banners proclaiming "You're almost there, champ!"

The biggest takeaway from the book, for our purposes, is just to know there *is* a dip awaiting you; that insight should give you at least some level of comfort and perhaps even a sense of control. It's sort of the reverse of the old story about the kid at Christmas who gets a pile of manure as a present and proceeds to gleefully dig into it. Why? Because "With all this poop, there's got to be a pony in here!" In the case of your journey, in the midst of sunlight, you can expect a dip is awaiting you at some point. When it appears, you can say, "Oh, there you are. I was wondering when you would show up." And then you're back in control!

To help you be preemptive, make a list of all the hiccups, hard stops, and harsh words you might encounter — particularly from your own head. Then, as these arise, just put a big-assed check mark next to it on your list and say, "In your face, buster! I saw you coming and I know how to deal with you."

What kind of dip or dips could be awaiting you?

How can you preempt them?

HOW TO GET UNSTUCK

Making a dip list is a great segue into six techniques that can help you get through whatever is holding you back. You don't have to apply them all, just use the ones that resonate for you. And if one of them makes you squirm, that's likely to be the most helpful!

Confront What You're Resisting

There is a popular phrase in the coaching world: *What you resist persists.* If you've been avoiding something — making a hard decision, saying "No," reaching out for help, or starting something you're not sure will work — it's time to get into action. Fear, uncertainty, and doubt rob you of energy, divert your focus, and make you feel even more stuck. So whether you're feeling blocked, discouraged, overwhelmed, or lost, it's time to step into your discomfort. Don't worry, you'll survive, and you'll be back in higher gear when you're on the other side.

This work starts with two questions:

1) *What are you resisting?*
2) *Why are you resisting this?*

To break through what's holding you back, you need to be honest with yourself and own the things you are hesitant to acknowledge. Until you can see clearly what is happening and how your thinking and behaviors are affecting your efforts, you will continue to be stuck.

Once you have an answer for #2 above, ask yourself: *Why is that a problem?* Once you have an answer to this third question, ask yourself: *Why is that a problem?*

By now, you'll be way past your answer from #2. It's not that what you came up with initially is irrelevant or off-base, it just wasn't deep enough. Here's an example:

1) *What are you resisting?* Speaking up for myself.
2) *Why are you resisting this?* I'm afraid of rejection.
3) *Why is that a problem?* Rejection makes me feel worthless.
4) *Why is that a problem?* It makes me feel like what I do doesn't matter.

The answer in #2, while deep and emotional, is not as exacting as that in #4. If you were working with a coach or therapist, for #2, they might challenge you to seek out small opportunities to face or even invite rejection just to build a capacity to handle it when the stakes increase. For the answer in #4, however, the coach or therapist might have you list all the ways you *do* matter and all the positive impact you've had on the world, and then build from there to a state of *you-can't-fuck-with-me* that makes rejection irrelevant.

(This can be deep, emotional work. If you're unsure about doing it on your own, get a coach or therapist to help you through the process.)

As you go through the questions, don't merely spin these ideas in your head, write them down or type them into a note; if you keep a journal, capture your discoveries there. Recording your answers gets all this out of your head so you can better process it; this also gives you a chance to see the progression of your thoughts.

As a last step, answer this: *How do you want to move forward?*

Having deep insights is one thing, but without deciding how to proceed and then taking action, you're not much further ahead. If you need time to let this work settle, take it. But don't pause so long that you let all that crap seep back into your thoughts; take a step forward, no matter how small, as a way to declare, "I've got this now!"

1) What are you resisting?

2) Why are you resisting this?

3) Why is your answer to #2 a problem?

4) Why is your answer to #3 a problem?

5) How do you want to move forward?

Redefine Failure

"Failure" is a tricky word. It is reviled by many, celebrated by some (in the startup community, "fail fast" is a rallying cry). But when it's your *life*, failure is rarely cheered. It is usually interpreted as you weren't good enough or lacked something important or made bad decisions or just got caught out at a bad time (or so you tell yourself).

Ultimately, the impact of the word depends on the power you grant it. If you think failure is bad, you'll feel all kinds of hurt if you're on the verge of failing at something; fear of failure might stop you from even beginning a new quest. Conversely, if you think failure is an essential part of your growth — if you embrace the idea that failure is *required* for you to grow, as Melissa Ford says in her book *Living Service* — then failures (if you even call them that) are to be embraced.

You see this all over the business world, where companies make lots of little bets, knowing that most of them will fail, but a few will be spectacular successes and will more than cover the costs of the failed efforts. This is how the venture capital world works, as well as companies like Alphabet (Google) and Apple, and entrepreneurs like Richard Branson. Thomas J. Watson, the founder of IBM, said this: "If you want to increase your success rate, double your failure rate."

So what if you turned "failure" into a game? What if you *allowed* yourself, even pushed yourself, to accumulate — to achieve! — a certain number of "fails" per week or month? What if you embraced failure, without recrimination, as a way to test the boundaries of what is really possible for yourself? If you're learning and growing and, in the process, getting smarter and more accomplished, don't those fails ultimately become successes?

I did this years ago with one of my sons, a very passionate, driven, elite-level soccer player. He would beat himself up when he made even the slightest mistake, and in the process would take himself mentally out of the game as he stewed in his seeming failure. After observing this several times, I finally sat him down for a chat. We talked about mistakes being a natural part of the game and of life, and we negotiated the number of flubs he would allow himself to have without beating himself up; he chose to allow himself three mistakes per game

(I lobbied for five). By putting aside the need to be perfect and avoid failure, this helped him play more freely and creatively.

Master coach Brooke Castillo did an episode (#279) on *Failure Tolerance* for her podcast. In it, she talks about increasing your tolerance for failure, and thus increasing your rate of learning and growth, by — guess what? — failing! This concept of failure tolerance is really powerful, particularly when your level is a 10 out of 10. At that point, there is no whining, complaining, finger pointing, or beating yourself up. It's just a continual state of experimentation, of trying things and (when not successful) saying "That didn't work? Okay, let's try *this.*" It's like Thomas Edison and his 10,000 failed attempts before finally getting the elements right to make a lightbulb. The more you ramp up the flywheel of learning, the more you're going to find your successes building faster and faster.

If you face a situation where things have gone bad and you want to stamp FAILURE all over it, shift your perspective from "I suck" to "I just learned something." Then take a page from David Goggins, who suggests doing three things: 1) recognize what went well; 2) be clear and nonjudgmental about your preparations, execution, and thinking during this failure; then 3) make a list of the things you can fix. This doesn't unwind what happened, but being honest with yourself and having a positive outlook on "growth experiences" (formerly known as "failures") will help you get back into action right away.

What could you do if your tolerance for failure was a 10?

What's stopping you from doing that right now?

Catalog Your Accomplishments

Sometimes it's hard to see yourself — really see yourself — when you're feeling blocked and things don't seem to be working. When you're struggling, your vision narrows and it can feel like you're stuck in a box.

At that moment, a shot of confidence can help you say, "Hell No!" to the box and its limitations. It can resuscitate your passion and drive, which is what you'll need to keep going.

One of the best ways to recover your footing and your belief in yourself is to catalog your accomplishments — at work, with family, in the world. Make as long a list as you can, filling it with every instance you can remember of times you fought for something, overcame adversity, believed in yourself when no one else did, and so on.

This shouldn't just be about titles you've attained, awards you've received, or good press you've gotten. The real richness is in those moments when you had to overcome obstacles to achieve your goals. Hell, even if you didn't "succeed" in a traditional sense, if you faced barriers and gave your all, that *is* success. So acknowledge that and add it to your list.

Another thing you should do is celebrate what you've already accomplished on *this* journey. If we use the metaphor of climbing a mountain, this is like pausing on the trail and looking back at how far you've come already. If you only look up at the still-faraway peak, and the wall of trees in front of you, it's easy to get overwhelmed. But when you take a moment to look back at how high you've climbed and consider all the rugged terrain you've already mastered, it should give you hope and energy for continuing your trek.

This reminds me of when I was preparing for my first marathon. In my training plan, on a particular weekend in January, I needed to do a 14-mile, race-pace run. Given how tightly defined was my build-up, this hard effort had to be done on that specific weekend, regardless of the weather. But the conditions in New York City were horrible the whole weekend, so I finally decided to do this indoors, on a treadmill.

If you've ever done any running on a treadmill, you know how numbing it can be. I embraced it anyway, because the goal of running my first marathon was unwavering. So I went to the dank, window-less room at my health club and began to run. It was as grueling as you might imagine. (Not as grueling as what David Goggins puts himself through, but few of us are in his class.) What got me through the 100 or so minutes it took to complete this was to focus on just the next five minutes of running. Once I passed the halfway point, I celebrated how much less I still had to run. This was in the days before health clubs had things to divert your attention, so all I had to look at was the big clock on the wall in front of me. Every five minutes, I celebrated, and that got me through an intense effort.

Cataloging and celebrating your accomplishments are powerful buffers when voices in your head try to tell you have no fucking reason to be doing what you're doing. Hell yes you do!

What can you celebrate about your journey so far?

Make a Game of It

Reinvention can be serious business, especially when you're confronting road blocks to your dream. So let's change the perspective that it's all hard work and turn it into a game. This is inspired by my friend and top coach, Melissa Ford, whom you met a few pages back. And there are two different ways you can play this game.

Early in her coaching career, while struggling to build her business, Melissa came up with a way to encourage herself to do the tasks she was resisting (e.g. reaching out to people to invite them into coaching conversations). She got a big glass jar and labeled it **The Scary Jar.**

She kept slips of paper, plus pens and markers nearby, and every time she did something she'd been resisting, she wrote her accomplishment on one of the slips of paper and put it in the jar.

Every day, she could see how the collection of scary things she'd conquered was growing; that's why it's important to have a glass jar — and a big one! Each of those slips of paper was testament to her increasing ability to handle things that she had previously resisted, and it strengthened both her resilience and her resolve, day by day by day. It is a brilliant solution to marking your progress, both in the casual glances at the jar as it fills *and* in the ability to go back through all those victories, large and small, when you need a shot of confidence. Melissa used The Scary Jar for more than two years, long after her business started to soar, because she loved the way it both challenged and supported her.

Of course, it's one thing to have a jar and slips of paper, and it's another to actually step up and do these hard things. Once Melissa had decided on this game, here's how she handled the scary moments. She would recognize what she needed to do, like having a difficult conversation with someone, and then she would jump right into it. No hesitation, no postponing it for some later date; she would just do it. This is kind of like Mel Robbins's *The 5-Second Rule*, where when you're facing something hard, you count down from 5 to 1 and then do it, only in Melissa's case, she jumped straight to 1.

Sure, you could do these things without playing the game, but having a structure like The Scary Jar actually makes it easier to face these challenges. You're just doing what you need to do for the game; no big deal. The accumulation of so many accomplishments helps to dilute the significance of any individual task you have to do. It's merely fodder for The Scary Jar.

There is one more step to Melissa's process, a subtle yet critical part to reinforcing your resolve. Once she had done the hard thing, and before she reached for paper and pen to memorialize it, she stopped and took a breath, just to make sure she was still alive. Yep, she'd survived what had previously seemed overwhelming. When we talked about The Scary Jar, she repeated this "Am I still alive?" check-in several times, so it's clear how integral this was to her approach.

While she labeled this as The Scary Jar, it could just as easily be called The Victory Jar or The Hell Yeah! Jar. One of her clients called it The Gratitude Jar, adding a wonderful dimension to the significance of these small, but hard efforts building up over time.

There's another way to play with The Scary Jar, which is what I imagined when Melissa first said those words to me. Instead of putting completed items into the jar, you would load the jar up with all the things you've been resisting and then take them out one at a time and do them.

Whatever it is you pull out of the jar, you are obligated to do it. You can't put things back in because you don't want to do them. You have to suck it up and take action. *Send out prospecting emails.* Ulp. Okay, I'll do it. *Call my accountant.* Ugh. Alright. *Talk with Mom about taking her meds consistently.* Yeah. That can't be postponed any longer.

This makes a game of Eleanor Roosevelt's quote: "Do one thing every day that scares you." It's in the discipline of pulling out a new item every day that helps develop your ability to step into these challenges, rather than away from them. You become stronger, more confident, and better able to handle what life throws your way.

One of the considerations with this second approach to The Scary Jar is in the timeliness of the items you're accumulating. You might be okay with some of them sitting in the jar for a while, but there are likely some that need to be addressed right away or before a particular deadline. You'll need to figure out what works for you regarding these considerations.

As well, you should pace yourself. It would be great if you could bash them all out in a day or two, but you might reach a level of burnout. So do one or two a day to start, then see how that feels — and how quickly the jar refills.

Perhaps the best way to merge these two games is to have a big-ass Scary Jar to accumulate all your triumphs, and a smaller Scary Dish next to it with the few things you need to do soon that you have been avoiding.

Ultimately, how you play the game is up to you, but take this as an invitation to do *something* in a structured way that will get you past those road blocks that are slowing your progress.

Get Creative

Here are two more approaches that are decidedly un-serious, but can have a huge impact in breaking through what's holding you back — making a drawing of your situation or writing about it.

Part of what makes your issues so formidable is uncertainty about them. What might *really* happen? Am I facing utter humiliation or financial ruin? Is this just an ego trip? Am I going to go too far down a road that could be a dead-end? Why is my progress so slow? What if no one likes what I'm doing?

Drawing or writing your story makes these challenges and threats more concrete. It helps you see them from new perspectives and gives you a sense of control you didn't otherwise have. As well, if you add a bit of humor to how you characterize what's holding you back, either in sketch form or words, you further defuse its power. Doing all this doesn't immediately vaporize the fear, uncertainty or doubt, but it makes it easier to move forward.

If writing or drawing seems frivolous to you, that's all the more reason to do this. If you're feeling blocked or held back, pushing harder using the same approach you've been employing is like stomping on the accelerator when your car is stuck in mud; you're only going to dig yourself in deeper.

To gain traction and get past what's holding you back, you need to take a new approach. So get some paper and a writing implement and let's see what new insights you can uncover.

Drawing

There's power in being able to *see* what your situation is like, not just spin it around in your head. Is it large and foreboding, or is it like some yappy little dog that's more annoyance than real threat. The more you can define it, almost like a police sketch artist, the easier it will be to gauge its true impact. Then you can take whatever steps you need to turn that situation to your advantage.

I realize this is outside the ordinary, but you've got to try it. To illustrate this, here's one of my big hurdles — reaching out to people I don't know.

I'll skip the painful backstory. The bottomline is that whenever I needed to approach someone I didn't know, particularly if I had to ask them for something, part of me went into lockdown. I could analyze this endlessly, but my body would just go "Nooooooooo!"

Here is how I imagined my dilemma . . .

My first thought after I drew this: what a fucking bully! Why is this guy so mean, when I've got something wonderful to give him? My next thought: I don't need to suck up to this guy. If he doesn't want my heartfelt offering, it's his loss not mine.

Of course, most people aren't bullies and my fear-mechanism didn't serve either the people I was reaching out to or myself. This image helps me remember that I don't need to be the small, fearful guy hoping not to be crushed by the big, bad bully. And if I don't approach situations *expecting* to be bullied, it creates opportunities to connect with people as equals. If they're interested in what I'm offering, great! If they're not, it's no big deal. I now have this image on my desk as a reminder of how I *can* be.

It's liberating to get your issues out of an endless loop in your head and into a form you can actually see and poke at and take action on. You might even have a conversation with it. Like, "Hey, Formerly-Scary-Monster, what's up? Why are you messing with my head and trying to hold me back? And do we really need to struggle with each other? Are you trying to protect me from something or are you just an asshole who enjoys seeing me suffer?" That could be an enlightening conversation!

In doing these drawings, artistic skill is not required and neatness doesn't count. It's about getting the right expression of your situation into a form you can examine. Consider this drawing:

Man, what a woeful state of affairs. This guy is on an endless road that looks like it's going to get complex and confusing, ending up in a horrible mess and falling down to nowhere. (And does the road turn into an alligator at one point? I can't unsee that now...)

It took me 60 seconds to make that drawing, yet it fully captures how the guy is stopped in his tracks and freaking out about the path ahead. Like "I'm *never* going to get there!" Which could be followed by "Why bother continuing on this road?" And, boom, he's out of the game.

When you can draw it out, as rough as this image is, you can look at it objectively and decide how to change your approach. If you were driving and had a bizarre road like this ahead of you, you'd probably at least pause and check out two things: 1) Is it really as messed up as it looks, or is my mind playing tricks on me? 2) If it really is the worst road in the world, what other route can I take to get past it? And if you really love to drive, there might be a third option: This road looks like a blast!

Let's do one more, to help you see how to do this. Remember our friend the labradoodle breeder? It seems like everything is hitting him at once. The mayor is threatening to drop approval to use City Park for the Autumn Dog Festival unless a huge deposit is paid. The school board is nervous about a teacher or child being bitten during the planned Dogs At School program and is ready to cancel it. Other breeders are trying to block our friend's access to the local directory of breeders. And his wife claims he pays more attention to the dogs than to her.

He feels like he's being bludgeoned and can't seem to find his way forward. So he sat down and made this drawing.

It's easy to lose perspective and a sense of priorities when you're hit by lots of things at once, each of which feels like the most urgent concern to address. By drawing this out, the breeder was able to take a step back and look at all the demands he was facing. Sure, it felt like every group wanted him to stop what he was doing, but other than the evil breeders, who were just spiteful, the rest only needed some clarity and assurance. So the breeder went to each of them (his wife first) and resolved their concerns. All thanks to a simple drawing that gave structure to his thoughts.

Getting issues out of your head and onto paper brings insight, clarity, and the opportunity to revise your plans if necessary. And it can start with just a goofy little sketch. Try it!

Writing

Writing gives you a chance to sort out that mass of ideas and issues swirling around in your brain. By committing your thoughts, hopes, and fears to paper or pixels, you remove them from the loop they've been in and you can start to connect the proverbial dots on what is really happening inside you. Writing lets you step back from all the noise and see the bigger picture of your situation.

There are several ways you can use writing to clear out your head. The first is just to do a stream-of-consciousness brain dump, where you write, write, write without any thought of structure or meaning, and then go back afterwards to find the threads or themes that will open up your understanding.

Another way is to write out a conversation with yourself and to see where the voices in your head lead you. It might go something like this:

1: Hey, John, what will it take to make a decision on this job?
2: An act of God?
1: Funny. Clearly, you're avoiding this. Why?
2: *deep sigh* I'm worried about screwing this up.
1: Okay, let's work on *that* for now…

If you try this approach, pay attention to the language these voices use with each other. If your voices are being abusive or defensive with each other, that could provide clues to why you're feeling blocked.

The simplest way to open up and organize your thinking is just to answer some questions, which you'll find below. It's critically important to write out your answers, not just spin them in your head. By committing these ideas to words and sentences, you will be crystallizing your thoughts. And you'll be able to build on these answers later, as they continue to dance around in your head.

What's blocking your progress?

What's the cost of not moving forward?

What's the benefit of not moving forward?

How long can you tolerate not making progress?

What other ways could you approach this situation?

What If It's Not Working Out?

What if you still feel completely blocked? You've done all the exercises above and you continue to be stuck. You're putting in effort, but not making progress. Or you keep getting "No"s and you're fed up with getting "No"s. Or you've lost the spark you'd had at first. Do you have to keep pushing, pushing, pushing forever?

No.

Just because you've invested a lot of time and perhaps money in what you've been pursuing doesn't mean you are obligated to keep going in that direction until you achieve your goal or die. As alluded to above by Ryan Holliday, there can be wisdom in going back to the drawing board. At any moment, you should make decisions about your future from where you are right now, not because of how much of yourself you've poured into it.

I had a long and painful experience with this. In 2010, I was seized by the new app store for iPhones and iPads. I designed an app for better, faster, fewer meetings and hired a group to do the coding. It was a big hit right away, with thousands of buyers at a premium price, across 81 countries. It even spent four weeks at the top of Apple's list of the best iPad apps for business.

My customers clamored for an integrated, desktop model, so I designed an expanded version. Since I had more than made back my initial investment, my wife and I decided to spend the money to get the new app built.

By then, I was working with a group in India. Their proposal said it would take three months and $28,000 to build this. I figured it might take twice that long and cost 30% more, but I gave them the go-ahead.

Their estimate was way off. It took *two years and three months*, and cost more than double the original projection. I worked 70-hour weeks to finish this and my wife was unhappy with the whole thing.

As months turned to years, the market shifted. Standalone apps like mine were replaced by sharing apps like Slack, and while Slack couldn't do a lot of what mine did, it was clear my opportunity had faded. I kept things going until the app was finished, but I shut it down shortly thereafter; no amount of money thrown at marketing was going to revive it. Shutting this down was one of the hardest things I've ever done — but it was the only sensible thing to do.

So, BIG effort, BIG expense, years poured into it, almost cost me my marriage, and then I shut it down when it was clear I couldn't make it successful. Did that mean I was a failure? Not at all. I just needed to find a new direction, and I eventually found that in coaching.

Don't lock yourself in when you know in your heart of hearts that something isn't going to work. You're not wrong for trying.

But if you're not sure whether you're in a dip or on a road to nowhere, how do you figure that out? Here's an approach I wish I had figured out back then.

First, if you're feeling stressed about what you're pursuing, don't jump into a rash decision. Unless you have deadlines or deliverables looming, take some time off. It could be a day or a week, or maybe even a month, but you want to get to the point where the mere thought of this doesn't put you into a fight-flight-or-freeze mode. If you take an ample break and you're still feeling tense, you're probably cooked and it's time to move on.

But if you step away for a little bit and find you can't wait to get back to it, then you're probably just in a dip. And it may be that you need to recalibrate, or to find a different way to pursue this. There's nothing magical about the first path you chose. What's magical is where you're going and, most importantly, *how you're feeling* during the journey. So answer these questions:

What still interests you about your original idea?

What are the reasons for stopping this pursuit?

What are the reasons for continuing to pursue it?

How would it feel to stop what you're pursuing?

How would it feel to search for a new direction?

Nobody said that reinventing yourself would be easy, but hopefully some of the techniques above have sparked new insights and recharged your momentum. We'll cover a few more things in the next chapter to help you settle into this new direction and make it last.

To distill everything we've covered in this chapter, embracing the struggle requires three things — conviction, courage, and creativity. (And persistence, optimism, resilience, and maybe a dozen other things; I was just having fun with the alliteration.)

Don't let anything stop you!

What are your biggest takeaways from this chapter?

What can you put into action TODAY?

Making It Last

*The secret to getting results that last
is to never stop making improvements.*
· James Clear ·

There is a 2900-foot, shear face in Yosemite, California on a massive rock formation called El Capitan. It's intimidating as hell just to look at it, and even climbers using ropes have a healthy fear of the climb. No one had ever completed a free-solo ascent of El Capitan — a climb done without ropes, crew, or safety apparatus — before Alex Honnold stepped up to the wall in June 2017.

Among climbers, Honnold is perhaps the most elite of the elite. His speciality is free-soloing slab-like rock faces, where one slip could lead to death. At a certain point in his career, he had done so many outlandish climbs that a major sponsor dropped him as a client because "these forms of the sport are pushing boundaries and taking the element of risk to a place where we as a company are no longer willing to go." So he was already extreme before he did the most extreme thing of all for a climber.

A film crew had been following him for months, documenting his intended climb. That became the film *Free Solo*, which won the Academy Award for Best Documentary in 2019. But early on June 3, 2017, the filmmakers almost missed the start of his historic ascent, as Honnold slipped silently to the base of El Capitan.

It took him 3 hours and 56 minutes to complete the climb. This has since been described as one of the greatest athletic achievements of any kind, ever. It was an epic feat and he has traveled the world telling his story.

As for his big passion, climbing, what do you do after something like that, when you've reached the pinnacle of your sport? Take up knitting?

In Honnold's case, he has continued to climb, seeking out other challenges, like setting speed records on super-difficult routes. He's also found other outlets to share his expertise, his love of the sport, and how to succeed when your life is truly on the line.

The lesson here is that life doesn't stop once you've reached your goal. In a way, you're just getting started. And if you keep that mindset, where you're now an ace on some new things and a beginner on others, you will keep rocking this thing we call life. You will wake up with curiosity about what you might discover today, you won't let setbacks crush you, you'll be having a great time, and you'll continue to be an inspiration to others.

So what do you do to keep the vibe going? Here are some ideas.

Do an Annual Review

How has your journey been? What are the highlights? Where have you struggled? If you did this over again, what would you do more of, and what would you do differently?

Doing a review like this celebrates your achievements, solidifies your vision, and fine tunes your ability to handle whatever else may come up in your life.

Some other questions to consider:

- What's different about you now?
- What are you capable of that you weren't before?
- How have your relationships changed?
- What have you felt excited about?
- What has been tough about the effort?

What has it taken to get you to this point?

What has gone particularly well?

What would you do differently next time?

Do Quarterly Check-ins

Since there's no finish line to this reinvention process, it's important to check on your progress now and then. Being aware of what's working and not working keeps you aligned with your goals and helps you recover more quickly if you're veering off course.

Here are the things to check yourself on:

- Am I still headed the direction I wanted to go?
- Am I feeling the way I wanted to be feeling?
- Am I having the impact I wanted to have?
- Am I still feeling motivated and engaged?
- When was the last time I celebrated something?
- Who could help me move forward?
- Who can I help?

For each of the answers to these questions, ask yourself *"How satisfied am I with that?"* It's a critical question. You don't have to have all "10s" for your life to feel good, but if something is off, it will help to find out sooner rather than later.

If your answers to how satisfied you are meet or exceed your expectations, yay you! Keep on with what you're doing. If, however, your satisfaction is not high for one or more of your answers, how you want to deal with that? If you just need a little course correction, aren't you glad you stopped to check in with yourself?

And if your satisfaction is low for one or more answers, it's time to dig in to see what's going on. Did you lose your focus at some point? Did your initial plans become too complicated or difficult to manage? Perhaps, over time, your enthusiasm has waned?

There's no dishonor is in changing to a new direction for your life, if that's what makes sense now. Take a moment to acknowledge what a great effort you've put in, then take some time to do nothing special. When you're ready, restart the reinvention process from the *Taking Stock* chapter.

As to when to do check-ins, start with every three months. You can lengthen the interval later if it feels too frequent, or shorten the interval if it seems too long between reviews.

How satisfied are you with your progress to-date?

Share What You've Learned

You know so much more now than you did before starting this journey — about yourself and about the process of change. Don't let all that go to waste. There are so many people, of all ages, who can benefit from the wisdom you have gained, not just in this reinvention stuff, but about life in general. You are a role model for what's possible when one dedicates themself to living fully. It's time to spread the news!

Stories not only lift others up, but also bring clarity to your own growth and what has mattered most in your journey. Telling your story will remind you of how far you've come and provide new perspectives to help you chart where you go next.

So get out there, literally or figuratively, and share yourself with the world. Whether that's in mentoring others, writing, teaching a class, or maybe just volunteering to read books to kids.

You have a story to tell. Please tell it.

The world needs your wisdom.

How can you share what you've learned?

How Do You Define Yourself Now?

"So, what do you do?"

How often have your heard that question? At social gatherings, business functions, or while sitting on a plane, it is the most frequent question people hear.

By now, you might have a ready answer that expresses what you're pursuing and how you've reframed your life. If so, great! If your reply leads to a rich discussion about reinventing one's life and how we should never settle for something less than full engagement, I'm really happy for you. You may now proceed to the last chapter.

If, however, you get stuck on that question, it's time to clear up the crap and put a big-assed stake in the ground for who you are now and what you're doing.

Let's start with the question itself: *So, what do you do?* It seems innocent and non-threatening, maybe even boring. Typically, that question is asked so the person can figure out how to classify you or decide what kind of box to put you in. In those scenarios, it almost doesn't matter what you say; they're just looking for *something* to ask, and this is the easiest question of all.

Sometimes, though, the question comes from a sincere desire to get to know you and what you bring to the world. For those occasions, take your cue from the last word in that query: "do."

Too often, we answer that question with who we *are* rather than what we *do*. We say, "I'm a doctor" or "I'm a teacher" or "I'm a CEO," rather than "I help people walk again" or "I expand kids' minds" or "I'm working to bring drug prices down." And if you no longer fill that role, too often the fast answer is "I *was* (a doctor, teacher, CEO, etc)."

What if, instead of giving people an easy label to slap on you, you answer with what you're actually doing? "I'm writing a book" or "I'm raising money to rebuild villages in Nepal" or "I'm doing *nothing* for six months, because I've earned that, and then who knows what the hell I'm going to do."

Those are conversation starters! Those practically demand, "Wow, tell me more." And in the process, you have switched from a curt, even defensive reply to something that invites a rich conversation — and invites the other person to share more of themselves in the process.

William Bridges, in *Transitions: Making Sense of Life's Changes*, talks about using a "participial" identity — using *ing* words (writing, running, lecturing, building) rather than nouns. Put another way, it's about using active verbs to define what you do, rather than turning yourself into a *thing* and preemptively sticking yourself into a box.

Ultimately, how you reply isn't about making it easy for new conversation partners or people you haven't seen in a while to classify you. This is about the stories you tell *yourself* regarding who you are and what you're doing with your life.

Are your stories stuck in your past or infused with what you're doing now? If you are passionate about what you're pursuing, it is effortless to say, "Here's what gets me out of bed every morning!"

But let's say you need *something* to put on a business card or your LinkedIn profile. Here are some ideas for our friend, the labradoodle breeder.

- TRADITIONAL: CEO, Big Dogs Ltd.
- PLAYFUL: Lounging with Labradoodles
- INTRIGUING: Building Communities, One Dog at a Time
- SUBLIME: Sharing Doodle Love with the World
- BORING: Dog Breeder

The traditional one might get a nibble of interest, since most people probably don't think about dogs being a big business. The boring approach would probably elicit "Oh, that's nice" before the other person bolts for another drink.

But the three approaches in the middle will definitely get someone to say, "What is that about?" And did you notice that the three options in the middle all started with active verbs? That's the approach to take.

Meanwhile, what's the place, if any, for what you did before? Do you even bring it up? Do you feature it? How much of a hold on your life *now* does your prior career have on you?

In my first career, I did a starring role on Broadway. It was only for one night, but that's still something that most people, even most actors, never achieve. As special as that experience was (and it has a great story around it), I never bring it up in conversation unless it is completely, compellingly relevant. All my other, prior personas — MBA, novelist, entrepreneur, and more — stay locked up, too, unless there's a solid reason to mention them.

How would that be for you? Can you leave the past to the past and focus on what you're doing now? The more you can look forward, the more fully engaged you can be with what's happening RIGHT. NOW.

Betty Friedan, in her book *The Fountain of Age*, tells the story of Hollywood producer Sam Jaffe, who at 85 joined a discussion group at UCLA called The Plato Society to meet with others 55 and older who just wanted to learn new things. In his own words, he knew he could "mesmerize" the others with his old Hollywood stories, but he never brought them up. Instead, he was just the new guy in the group and anxious to learn about things he had never studied.

Give yourself the gift of just being You. The only person you have to impress is yourself.

How do you define yourself now?

A Few Words on Legacy

What you leave behind is not what
is engraved in stone monuments,
but what is woven into the lives of others.
· Pericles ·

When I was 12, a new family moved in across the street. A few weeks later, my mom invited them to our house for dinner. After the adults introduced themselves, they gestured to their 8-year old daughter and said, "This is Melanie. We hope everyone will refer to her as 'Lanie.'"

I remember thinking, "The kids at school are definitely going to call her 'Mel.'" And that's exactly what happened.

It's the same when it comes to your legacy. You can have great aspirations for how you want to be remembered, but the legend of your life is not in your hands. It is shaped and stamped by others.

Sure, if you have tons of money and make big donations, a lot of people will be helped by your gifts, and that's great. But how they think of you is decided by them, not you.

This doesn't mean legacies are bullshit and you can ignore them. You can't. You will have a legacy whether you are intentional about it or not.

The underlying questions for many people, in thinking about their legacy, are "Did I matter? What kind of difference did I make?"

For existential questions, these shoot right to the top.

So let's go there. How have you mattered so far? Whose lives has been affected by you and what you've done?

If you ponder this, you're likely to come up with lots of people — your family, your friends, your colleagues at work, the people you have served through your profession and your community. As well, there are ripple effects from those you've affected directly to the people *they* have affected, thanks to your influence. Or people who have come across things you've written or donations you've made or people you've mentored or . . . the list could be endless. You may never be able to catalog all the people and all the ways you have made a difference in the world, and all the difference you still can make.

And that's where I'd like to draw your attention. Rather than think about a proclamation others may make about you after you're gone, or that you might make about yourself in your waning years, which is how most people envision a legacy, what if you focus just on today and how you can serve others?

If you think about how you can have an impact on others' lives today, and you repeat this every day until your last, you will build and burnish an amazing legacy that anyone could be proud of.

But better than that, better than having something to feel proud about, is how deeply alive and connected you will have been for all those days, and that will be the best example — and the best gift you can give — of a life well-lived.

How can you have an impact today?

(Repeat daily)

Parting Thoughts

I'm still learning.
· Michelangelo, at age 87 ·

Here we are, finally at the end, though really this is just the beginning. You have so much ahead of you!

If you've gone through this and done all the work, I hope you have found the process worthwhile. I imagine it hasn't always been easy, and that's not a bad thing. A caterpillar doesn't turn into a butterfly without some serious effort.

If you've done a first pass through the book and are ready now to really dig in, please take your time. There are marvelous things ahead of you and you need to give them the space to develop fully.

I'd love to hear about your experiences with this book and your process of reinvention. You can reach me at HiJohn@johnwindsor.co

Thanks so much for letting me help you in this journey. Your attention is a gift for which I am truly grateful. You can light up the world if you let yourself. Please, please do.

John

APPENDIX

Resources

Let's be brave enough to dream big, huge,
embarrassingly impossible dreams.
· Melody Ross ·

Below are resources you should investigate, if you want to deepen your understanding of aging, ageism, reinvention, and how to optimize your life in your later years. Some of these were mentioned in the body of the book and some are new here. These are among the sources that had the biggest impact on me.

First up, though, are PDFs for the exercises, for those reading this on a digital device, plus some information about coaching.

EXERCISES (download at johnwindsor.co/exercises)
- PDF of the full set of exercises
- 10/10/10 form
- Commitment Matrix
- PDF of links from this chapter

COACHING
Making a significant change in your life is hard to do alone. Working with a coach or a therapist can help you see yourself from new perspectives, with a partner who can support you when the road gets rough and challenge you when it seems like you're letting yourself

down. It's rarely a fast process, but working with someone who is an advocate for your highest dreams and expectations is one of the surest way to achieve lasting change.

If you're curious about what it would be like to work with a coach, I'd love to talk with you. You can find out more about coaching with me at johnwindsor.co

BOOKS

It would be so easy to dump a long list of books on you, and you might then not read any of them because where would you start? Here are some books worth your time and attention.

What Retirees Want by Ken Dychtwald & Robert Morison — This book offers a high-level view of the retirement landscape today, with compelling statistics about what older people are experiencing.

Growing Bolder by Marc Middleton — A far-ranging book, it takes a practical approach to beating ageism and living fully to your final days.

Successful Aging by Daniel Levitan — This book by a noted neuroscientist is loaded with insights about how to deal with aging. His #1 recommendation: Never retire.

This Chair Rocks by Ashton Applewhite — This "Manifesto Against Aging" is a take-no-prisoners look at ageism and how to beat it.

Wisdom @ Work by Chip Conley — Filled with practical advice, this book launched Conley's "Modern Elder" empire.

Code of the Extraordinary Mind by Vishen Lakhiani — This introduces the concept of "brules" (bullshit rules) as well as others like "Be unfuckwithable."

Atomic Habits by James Clear — This was a runaway bestseller on how to master habit change. It's a very enjoyable read.

Tiny Habits by B.J. Fogg — This is perhaps the best book on habit change, written by a Stanford professor.

The China Study by T. Colin Campbell — This is one of the key books on the importance of a plant-based diet.

Can't Hurt Me by David Goggins — The arc of Goggins's life and how he approaches adversity are spellbinding. If you want to learn about commitment, read this.

VIDEOS

Just as with books, I could bury you in things to watch. Here are some of the best.

What If Age Is Just a State of Mind by Bruce Grierson (TEDTalk) — This talk, in support of Grierson's book, *What Makes Olga Run*, was my introduction to Olga Kotelko. To see videos of Olga's exploits, go to YouTube.com and search on Olga Kotelko.

How to Die Young at a Very Old Age by Nir Barzilai (TEDTalk) — This particularly focuses on increasing our health span, not just our lifespan. The story of Irving Kahn and his siblings, starting at 6:50 in the video, is remarkable.

Is Retirement Bad for Your Brain? by Ross Andel (TEDTalk) — This covers some of the hidden dangers of retirement and how to mitigate them.

If You're Not in the Obit, Eat Breakfast (HBO) — This documentary features people in their 80s and above who are doing exceptional things.

Impossible Dreamers (Amazon Prime) — Similar to the "Obit" documentary, this profiles people who are not deterred by their age.

The Game Changers (Netflix) — This is a powerful, science-backed exploration of the benefits of a plant-based diet. Some of the results will shock you.

Failure Doesn't Exist by Kobe Bryant (YouTube) — This is a deep dive on how Kobe used to approach challenges in basketball and life.

Do What You Can't and **Make It Count** (YouTube) — These two videos by Casey Neistat are off-the-charts when it comes to following your own path and thinking outside the box. When I need a creative boost, I watch these!

WEBSITES

livingto100.com — life expectancy calculator from Thomas Perls

oldschool.com & **Yoisthisageist.com** — anti-ageism resources from Ashton Applewhite

modernelderacademy.com — self-discovey retreats from Chip Conley

growingbolder.com — all things on aging-with-style from Marc Middleton

agewave.com — insights on what's happening in the aging landscape from Ken Dychtwald

encore.org — new perspectives on how we live our lives now

nextavenue.org — a great resource for the myriad of experiences people are having as they age

ONLINE COURSE & MASTERMINDS

For information on the *F*ck Retirement* online course and mastermind groups, visit johnwindsor.co

More Profiles in Badassery

Tell me, what is it that you plan to do
with your one wild and precious life?
· Mary Oliver ·

In the course of writing this book, I came across many remarkable stories of people who have not let the specter of aging stop them from having an amazing life — particularly after reaching the so-called "retirement age."

These include centenarian athletes like French cyclist Robert Marchand, who was still setting records at 107, and Julia Hawkins and Diane Friedman, who were trading running records in the 100-104 age group. Plus social media influencers like 99-year old blogger Doris Carnevali, Woody Wilson (@funkygeezershow) who at 72 has almost 3 million followers for his music videos on TikTok, and "Angry Grandpa" Charles Green, who had 4.6 million subscribers who clicked his videos more than 1.5 billion times just to see him lose his shit.

And artists and activists and business executives who are still going strong as they near 100. As I write this, Warren Buffet continues to build his legacy at 91.

I could give you fifty pages of these stories, but that wouldn't capture them all. What follows is a small collection of people you should know about, as you consider what is and isn't possible for you in this next chapter of your life.

(1) Ida Keeling was 67 years old and drowning in depression over the deaths of her two sons in a short span of time. To help her try to shift her mood, Ida's daughter Shelley suggested that they go for a run together. The run turned out to be a 5k organized race, and Ida was hooked. She began running regularly, supplemented by 30 minutes a day of resistance training and an exercise bike, and started setting national age group records at the meets in which she participated. In 2016, she became the first woman in history to complete a 100-meter run at the age of 100. Her feat was witnessed by over forty thousand people at the prestigious Penn Relays. She lived to be 106 years old and was running almost to the end.

Ida's story and 16 more are part of an **HBO** documentary called *If You're Not in the Obit, Eat Breakfast.* Released in 2017, this wonderful film is hosted by then 95-year old Carl Reiner. If you're searching for inspiration, you have to watch this.

(2) You may not know the name Merry Clayton, but you've almost certainly heard her voice. Considered one of the greatest backup singers ever, she is best known for her explosive vocals on the Rolling Stones' classic recording "Gimme Shelter." She was also one of the stars of the Oscar-winning documentary, "20 Feet from Stardom."

But four months after the film won that award, at age 64, Merry was in a horrible auto accident that required amputating both her legs below the knee. As reported in a New York Times profile, when she got the news about her legs, her first question was "Did anything happen to my voice?" Eight years later, at age 72, she released her first album in 25 years. The name of the album? *Beautiful Scars.*

(3) The IRONMAN World Championship in Kona, Hawaii is a grueling affair for even the most fit creatures on the planet. To gain entry to this exclusive event, you have to place highly in your age group at sanctioned events. So if you're one of the 2500 competitors in Kona each October, you are among the most elite of endurance athletes. Even so, up to 10% of the entrants don't complete the race each year, either because of mechanical or physical problems, or because they can't finish the 2.4 mile swim, 112 mile bike ride, and 26.2 mile run in the allotted 17 hours.

Remarkably, in the 2018 race, Hiromu Inada of Japan finished the race in 16 hours, 53 minutes, and 50 seconds — at 85 years of age! He didn't do his first, much shorter triathlon until he was 70.

To further strip you of I-can't-do-it-itis, there's Fauja Singh of India, who started life as a sickly child and didn't walk until he was five years old. He got the running bug later in life and completed his first marathon at age 89. At 104, he ran the Mumbai Marathon.

(4) Ballet is an exacting art form, demanding poise, power, grace, explosiveness, musicality, and incredible athletic abilities. Women have the added challenge of doing this in pointe shoes, which requires even greater balance and control than the men are required to attain. To do this as a young person is difficult. Imagine if you were 81… That's Suzelle Poole.

Suzelle started in ballet at age 7 in London and hasn't stopped dancing since. After traveling the world, performing and teaching ballet, she settled in Dallas, Texas where she teaches classes six days a week — and still laces up her pointe shoes. In pictures, she looks as strong and as graceful as she was sixty years ago. And to see an 81-year old woman on pointe? Wow.

(5) Writing one book is a major undertaking. Writing dozens of books and becoming a legend in your field? You can't plan on that. For those that do become legends, their legacy is built one day at a time — one page, one chapter, one book, one lecture, and so on. One such man was Peter Drucker.

Drucker was among the most prolific and revered writers in the world of business. His 39 books have been translated into more than 36 languages. And here's the juicy part — he wrote 25 books after the age of 65. He published *nine* books in the final ten years of his life, from ages 85 to 95! Imagine what we would've missed out on if he'd retired in the traditional sense in his mid-60s.

(6) Management guru Mihaly Csikszentmihalyi, in his book *Creativity*, has this wonderful collection of later life achievers in his chapter on Creative Aging: "Guiseppe Verde wrote *Falstaff* when he was 80, and that opera is in many ways his best — certainly very different in style than anything ever written before. Ben Franklin invented the bifocal lens when he was 78. Frank Lloyd Wright completed the Guggenheim Museum when he was 91. Michelangelo was painting the striking frescoes in the Pauline chapel of the Vatican at 89. So although performance in many areas of life may peak in the 20s, the ability to contribute to the culture may actually increase in the later years."

(7) Continuing to learn new things is important for keeping your mind sharp. But how many older people would willingly step into a college class where the average age is 20? In her book, *Mindful Aging*, Andrea Brandt details the story of Nina Ochs, who paused her college career for over 70 years, finally getting her bachelor's degree at age 95 — graduating alongside her 21-year old granddaughter. She got her master's degree at 98 and was a graduate teaching assistant on her 100th birthday. Who says you're too old to learn?

(8) Masako Wakamiya from Japan, at age 81 became the oldest person to launch an app for iPhones and iPads. She didn't just dream it up, then have someone else design it and write the software (like I did), she actually taught herself how to code! That's a huge undertaking at any age, but to do it in her late 70s? She got her first computer at age 58, shortly before her retirement from a bank. Now she travels the world giving keynotes about aging and financial inclusion. She's also set up an investment fund for older folks to help young people start their own businesses. So, she became a software engineer, an entrepreneur, and a keynote speaker long after she had ended her traditional career.

(9) Vera Jiji loved playing the cello when she was young, but as she reached adulthood, the cello was moved to the back of her closet. Finally, at age 62, after retiring from a long career as a university professor, she pulled the cello out of her closet and began to play again — and is still playing more than 30 years later.

In a wonderful feature on her life in the New York Times, she talks about rekindling her love affair with cello and the amazing community she is a part of as a musician. At age 79, she wrote and published a book on playing cello. Now, at 93, she said, "Getting older doesn't mean you can't have something, you can. And getting older doesn't mean getting worse. I'm about enjoying the moment. You have to get up each morning and do something you love."

(10) One of the final stories from Carl Reiner's HBO documentary was about a man named Jim Martin, who was a paratrooper during D-Day, did a tandem jump in his 90s during a D-Day ceremony, and who at 95 still split wood on his farm, using a 40-year old splitter he built himself. As he threw heavy sections of logs into the splitter, he talksed about his view of aging.

"The age part is nothing," he said. "I don't feel any different today than I did when I was 25 years old. People ask me what has contributed to me living a long time. I tell them — no tobacco, no alcohol, and lots of good sex."

To wrap this up, here's a priceless quote from Dr. Mario Martinez's book, *The MindBody Self*:

"I asked a 100-year-old woman how she would respond if people tell her that she's too old to do something she loves. She said, 'I'd tell them to fuck off!'"

About the Author

The arc of my life has been broad. From Broadway actor to MBA and international business executive in London, to novelist and stay-at-home dad for two babies, then back to business as VP of Marketing for a Silicon Valley startup. From there, I went to Boulder, Colorado where I've gone from presentation coach and top 5 blogger to app developer to, finally, a business and life coach.

Despite those big shifts, it's amazing how they have all contributed to the work I'm doing now, and to the ideas and exercises in this book. Of course, not everything could make it into the book — the story of my one night starring on Broadway and my crazy experience with marijuana-infused brownies are pretty entertaining, but had no real purpose in theses pages. When I dig deep, however, I can see a thread that links one path to the next to the next to the next, leading inexorably to my typing these words right now.

I'm sure you have similar threads in your own life, waiting to be revealed and shared.

"Torch Day"

Back in the mid-90s, I wrote two thrillers. Got an agent, didn't get a publisher, so they never made it into print and eventually I went back into the workforce. Fast forward to 2016 and I decided to self-publish the second of those two books, *Torch Day*. Written in 1995, it's about a shadowy militia leader and an outlaw hacker coming together to bring down the U.S. government. The climax of the story is frighteningly similar to what happened in Washington, D.C. on January 6, 2021. And the cover of the book, with the U.S. Capitol building in flames, looks just like photos of the Capitol under siege, taken twenty-five years later. If you're interested, you can find the book on Amazon at https://amzn.to/3DUrNt8.

Where to Find Me

If you'd like to connect or just stay in touch with new ideas I'm bringing to the world, go to johnwindsor.co and you'll find links to all my social feeds.

Acknowledgments

This book owes a huge debt to a lot of people. In fact, the more I think about those who helped shape my experiences and insights, the longer the list gets. But I'll keep this short.

The most important person in all of this has been my wife, Katrin, who gave me the support, encouragement, and space to create this book. If she hadn't said, "Sure, honey, go ahead and write it," this book might not have happened. She also got me into coaching in the first place, which has been such a gift. Thanks, my love!

My friend, Ravya, was a big influence. Not only was she the Accountability Buddy I mention in the book, but her unstinting advice and deep insights helped me find the right path when I sometimes veered off course. Thank you, dear friend.

My amazing coach, Lisa, helped me see myself and my mission clearly, when doubt or uncertainty started to pick at my resolve. Everyone should be so lucky to have someone like Lisa in their corner.

The Boulder Public Library system provided easy access to an incredible number of books that helped me develop what you're holding in your hands. If they gave an award for most books checked out in a year, I would've been a finalist two years in a row.

So many authors in the realm of aging and reinvention helped me refine my thinking, including Ken Dychtwald, Marc Middleton, Chip Conley, Ashton Applewhite, Vishen Lakhiani, and David Goggins. And podcasters like Rich Roll, Tim Ferriss, and Brooke Castillo, whose guests and ideas sparked new ways to think about life and change.

As well, there are authors who have shaped how I think about writing, helping me see what can be done with words, as well as the joy that this work creates. Chief among these are Elmore Leonard, Christopher Moore, and Jen Sincero.

I have OneDesigns at 99Designs.com to thank for the awesome cover design. He absolutely nailed how I've thought about this concept.

My clients have been a source of inspiration and joy. Even when the work is deep and hard, the wisdom of the moment shows us a brighter version of how each of us can be. My gratitude to you is endless.

Though neither of them had a direct influence on this book, my two sons, Bryan and Dan, fill me up in ways too numerous to count. I am a better human being, a better man, and a better coach because of you guys.

Finally, I want to thank you, dear reader, for your time and attention. You could have spent your energy and interest on other things; I am honored that you have chosen to spend them with me. I sincerely hope you have found this worthwhile.

Made in United States
North Haven, CT
18 November 2021

11263136R00134